SOFT-WARE IN 30 DAYS

SOFT- WARE IN 30 DAYS

How Agile Managers
Beat the Odds, Delight
Their Customers,
and Leave
Competitors
In the Dust

KEN SCHWABER and JEFF SUTHERLAND

WILEY

John Wiley & Sons, Inc.

Published by John Wiley & Sons, Inc., Hoboken, New Jersey.
Published simultaneously in Canada.

For general information on our other products and services or for technical support, please contact our Customer Care Department within the United States at (800) 762-2974, outside the United States at (317) 572-3993 or fax (317) 572-4002.

Wiley publishes in a variety of print and electronic formats and by print-on-demand. Some material included with standard print versions of this book may not be included in e-books or in print-on-demand. If this book refers to media such as a CD or DVD that is not included in the version you purchased, you may download this material at http://booksupport.wiley.com. For more information about Wiley products, visit www.wiley.com.

Library of Congress Cataloging-in-Publication Data:

Schwaber, Ken.
    Software in 30 days: how Agile managers beat the odds, delight their customers, and leave competitors in the dust/ Ken Schwaber, Jeff Sutherland.
        p. cm.
    Includes index.
    ISBN 978-1-118-20666-9 (pbk.); ISBN 978-1-118-22854-8 (ebk); ISBN 978-1-118-24090-8 (ebk);
    ISBN 978-1-118-26574-1 (ebk)
    1. Agile software development. 2. Scrum (Computer software development) 3. Computer software– Development. I. Sutherland, Jeffrey Victor. II. Title. III. Title: Software in thirty days.
    QA76.76.D47S3223 2012
    005.1–dc23

                                                                                            2011050969

Printed in the United States of America

V10018868_052820

To Ikujiro Nonaka, Babatunde A. Ogunnaike, and
Hirotaka Takeuchi for their inspiration and guidance.

Contents

About the Authors

Jeff Sutherland and Ken Schwaber are the creators of Scrum, a software development process that delivers software functionality in 30-day increments. Scrum was born when Jeff and Ken presented a paper at the OOPSLA conference in Austin, Texas, in August 1995. This paper, "Scrum Development Process," was the result of their collaboration prior to that point. The works of H. Takeuchio and I. Nonaka in their seminal works on lean knowledge creation, bottom-up intelligence, and teamwork had profoundly influenced Jeff. Babatunde Ogunnnike had profoundly influenced Ken in his work on industrial process control and the applicability of complexity theory and empiricism to software development.

In addition to being Scrum's creators, Jeff and Ken have also served as its wards. With their guidance, Scrum has evolved over time; more recently, they have developed ways to speed up Scrum's systematic evolution based on community experience and input. In "The Scrum Guide," found in Appendix 2 of this book, Jeff and Ken offer the complete definition of Scrum.

Dr. Jeff Sutherland is the chief executive officer of Scrum Inc., in Cambridge, Massachusetts, offering training, guidance, and coaching to companies across the globe. Jeff is a distinguished graduate of the United States Military Academy and a Top Gun of his USAF RF-4C Aircraft Commander class. Jeff has advanced degrees from Stanford University and a PhD from the University of

Colorado School of Medicine. He is also a senior advisor to OpenView Venture Partners, helping them implement Scrum and agile practices in all their portfolio companies. Jeff has extended and enhanced Scrum at many software companies and information technology (IT) organizations over the years.

Ken Schwaber is a software development professional, having spent the past 40 years of his life as a programmer, analyst, consultant, product manager, and business owner. Early in his career, Ken tried unsuccessfully to make waterfall software projects successful; he later developed an alternative to waterfall. Ken has spent the past 20 years developing Scrum and working with organizations around world to help them take advantage of it. Ken is one of the original signatories of the Agile Manifesto and the founder of the Agile Alliance and the Scrum Alliance. He is currently working to improve the software profession through Scrum.org. Ken and his wife, Christina, live in the Boston area. He is a graduate of the United States Merchant Marine Academy and has completed additional study in computer science at the University of Chicago and in business at the University of California at Los Angeles Anderson School of Management.

Acknowledgments

THIS BOOK WOULD not be what it is without the excellent copyediting of Arlette Ballew, the overall direction of Richard Narramore, and the laser focus of Carey Armstrong.

Introduction

WE, JEFF AND Ken, have been in the software industry, collectively, for 70 years. We have been software developers, managers in IT organizations and software product companies, and owners of both product companies and service organizations. More than 20 years ago, we created a process that lets organizations deliver software better. Since then, we have helped hundreds of organizations do the same. Our work has spread further than we have ever imagined possible, being put to use by millions of people. We are humbled by the extent of its adoption, and we are awed by the feats people have accomplished using it.

This is not the first book we have written on the topic of building software. It is, however, the first book we have written for people who do not themselves build software. This book is instead for leaders within organizations that depend on software for their survival and competitiveness. It is for leaders within organizations that can benefit from developing software rapidly, incrementally, and with the best return on investment possible. It is for leaders who face business and technological complexity that has made the delivery of software difficult. We have written this book so that these leaders can help their organizations achieve these goals, enhance their internal capabilities, improve their product offerings, and more.

This book is for chief executive officers (CEOs), executives, and senior managers who need their organizations to deliver better software in less time, with lower cost, greater predictability, and lower risk. For this audience, we have a message: You may have had negative experiences with software development in the past, but the industry has turned a corner. The software profession has radically improved its methods and its results. The uncertainty, risk, and waste to which you are accustomed are no longer par for the course. We have worked with many software organizations that have already turned the corner; we want to help you do so, too.

In this book, we show you how to create business value using a process that delivers complete pieces of software functionality at least every 30 days. This book will show you how you can prioritize the functionality you want and have it delivered á la carte. It will show you how to gain transparency not only into business value, by tracking functionality delivered against functionality desired, but also into the health of the software development process and your organization as a whole. The tools in this book will help you work with your software organization to get up to speed with modern practices and begin to deliver the results you've been expecting all along.

This is software in 30 days.

SOFT-WARE IN 30 DAYS

SECTION

I

Why Every Business in the World Can Produce Software in 30 Days

WE REACH OUT to every leader in an organization who wants to build better software products with better value and predictability. The software industry is turning around and radically improving. The uncertainty, risk, and waste you are used to are no longer necessary. We have 20 years of data under our belts from working with the many organizations that have already turned the corner. We want you to do so also. We want you to be able to build valuable, quality software predictably with manageable risk.

We reach out to you for two reasons. First, you have been ill served by the software industry for 40 years—not purposefully, but inextricably. We want to restore the partnership. Second, software is no longer only in the back room. Software is everywhere, in more and more critical operations of our society. We want you to be able to build software that we can all reliably depend on.

We hope we achieve our goals for this book. Regardless, do not give up. You no longer need to accept the terrible software results of the past. Move on.

In this part of the book, we investigate why software development has been so bad. We move on to show how software has improved and the two

1

underlying epiphanies that have facilitated this. We then show you how you can pilot our approach, and what you can do to help it succeed. Section II provides you with increasingly rigorous steps to take advantage of our new approach, should the pilot convince you to do so.

1

The Crisis in Software:
The Wrong Process Produces the Wrong Results

YOUR ORGANIZATION—WHETHER business, governmental, or nonprofit—likely needs to be able to create value by building, customizing, and using software. Without software, your ability to achieve your goals as a business leader is inherently limited, if not impossible. But despite this need, software development has historically been an unreliable, costly, error-prone endeavor.[1] This leaves you in a pickle: You need software, but you can't get what you need, when you need it, at a cost that is acceptable, at a level of quality the makes it usable.

Indeed, the Standish Group's 2011 CHAOS Report found that more than half of software projects conducted between 2002 and 2010 were either described as challenged or complete failures; just 37 percent were classified as successful (Figure 1.1) The Standish Group modestly defined a successful project as delivering all the requested functionality, on the expected date, for the

---

[1] April 11, 2005, Forrester Report "Corporate Software Development Fails to Satisfy on Speed or Quality." Corporate development shops continue to disappoint: A fall 2004 Forrester survey of 692 technology influencers—those who hold the information technology (IT) purse strings—indicated that nearly one-third are dissatisfied with the time it takes their development shops to deliver custom applications, and the same proportion is disappointed by the quality of the apps that are ultimately delivered. One-fifth of respondents are unhappy on both counts.

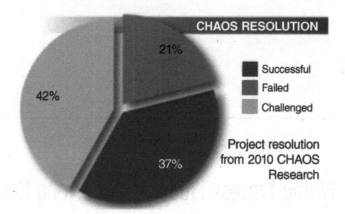

Figure 1.1   Traditional Software Development Is Risky

planned cost. The ability to accommodate changes, the ability to manage risks, or the inherent value of the software weren't considered.

The chances that a software project will be successful are not good. If you are trying to accomplish something critical that involves developing of software, you are probably worried. The software industry has failed you by being slow, expensive, and unpredictable. If software weren't so important, you would probably stop investing in software altogether.

You are not alone. Many others are in the same boat. For example, the Federal Bureau of Investigation's (FBI) Sentinel project recently ran into trouble. The FBI turned Sentinel around using the insights and processes described in this book.

The information here concerning Sentinel comes from the Department of Justice Inspector General reports, and it is publicly available. Before you dismiss this as a corner case, a particularity of government work, think about this: If a large government agency can radically improve how it builds software, then so can your organization.

Case Study: The FBI's Sentinel Project

Every FBI investigation has a case file that contains all of the records that were either created or obtained as part of an investigation. In 2003, the FBI decided to digitize cases and automate the related processes . . . Agents would then rapidly compare cases and discover connections between them. The name of the project was Sentinel.

In March 2006, the FBI initiated development of Sentinel, targeting an end-user base of more than 30,000 FBI agents, analysts, and administrative employees. Original estimates for Sentinel were $451 million to develop and deploy by December 2009. According to the FBI's original plan, Sentinel was to be developed in four phases. The FBI contracted the work to Lockheed Martin. Lockheed Martin proposed using a traditional software development process.

But by August 2010, the FBI had spent $405 million of the $451 million Sentinel budget but delivered the functionality for only two of Sentinel's four phases. Although these deliverables did improve the FBI's case management system, they did not deliver much of the value that was originally envisioned. Because of the cost and timeline overages, the FBI issued a stop-work order in July 2010 that directed Lockheed Martin to halt all work on the two remaining phases of Sentinel.

To this point, the FBI had been using a traditional development process, and it now chose to adopt a new approach to see if it could obtain better results. We developed this new process, called Scrum, in the early 1990s. The same Standish Group CHAOS Report that classified just 37 percent of projects as successful demonstrated how different the results of a traditional approach are versus those of using an agile, or Scrum, approach (Figure 1.2);

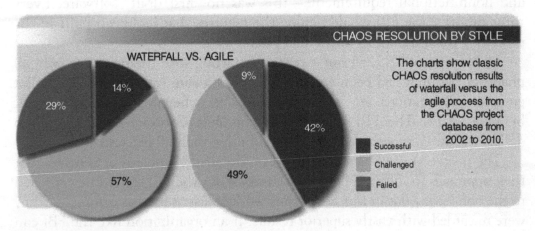

Figure 1.2 Agile Projects Are 3 times as Successful

specifically, it noted that whereas only 14 percent of traditional projects succeeded, a full 42 percent of projects using an agile approach achieved success. We argue that in addition to the Standish Group's traditional definitions of success, these projects also enabled greater responsiveness to changing customer needs, allowed for better risk mitigation, and ultimately delivered better-quality software.

By 2009, the FBI recruited a new chief information officer (CIO) and chief technology officer (CTO) with experience managing organizations that built software using our approach. They decided to see if this more agile approach could help the FBI. In 2010, the CTO told the Department of Justice that he was going to change the approach for Sentinel. He asserted that this new approach would streamline decision-making processes and allow the FBI to deliver Sentinel within budget. The FBI told the Inspector General at the Department of Justice that it believed it would be able to complete Sentinel with the remaining Sentinel budget and within 12 months of recommencing. An audit conducted by Mitre had previously concluded that the FBI would need an additional $35 million and six more years if it had continued with its traditional approach.

The FBI moved the entire Sentinel project to the basement of the FBI building in Washington, DC, and reduced the Sentinel staff from 400 to 45 people, 15 of whom were programmers. The CTO ran the project himself, managing toward a goal of delivering some of Sentinel's functionality every 30 days. Each increment of functionality had to meet all of the final functional and nonfunctional requirements—this was no "first draft" software. Every three months, the FBI would deploy the features that had been built in the preceding three iterations into a field pilot.

By November 2011, within a year of restarting with the new approach, all phases of Sentinel had been completed. The software was deployed to a pilot group of FBI locations, and remaining offices are scheduled to see deployment by June, 2012. The FBI was able to complete Sentinel for $30 million dollars within 12-months, a cost savings of more than 90 percent.

The people at the FBI worked hard on the first few phases of Sentinel, but their approach to software held them back. After the FBI shifted its approach to the one we lay out in this book, they worked just as hard as before, but they were rewarded with vastly superior results. If an organization like the FBI can do this, why can't yours?

The Wrong Approach: Predictive Processes

The process that the FBI originally used for Sentinel was what we refer to as a predictive, or sequential design, process. In fact, until 2005, the majority of software projects used predictive processes. Don't get us wrong; there are certainly circumstances in which predictive processes are more appropriate and could be successful. These circumstances, however, were the exception rather than the rule. If one can establish a complete vision, define all of the requirements of the vision, and then devise the detailed plan to turn the requirements into the vision, then a predictive process will work. But any deviation from the original vision, requirements, or plan creates great project risk. And with business needs and technology changing as rapidly as they do, it is rare that these elements can actually remain static. As a result, and as the Standish Group has reported, 86 percent of the software projects that use predictive processes are not successful. In fact, we consider the use of predictive processes to be the most common cause of problems in software projects.

The organizations that we work with have typically been struggling to increase the success rates for their software projects. They seek our help because they fear that their software organizations are spinning out of control. Their existing process has failed them, and they do not know of an alternative. Their problems with software development create a tremendous amount of waste for their organization, yet they persist because they are dependent on software to remain competitive.

Here is how the executives and managers typically describe the problems they are facing:

1. *Releases take longer and longer.* "Each release is taking more time, effort, and cost to get delivered to its customer(s). Several years ago, a release might have taken 18 months. That same release now takes us 24 months to develop, package, and deploy. Even then, a release is stressful and requires significant effort. We keep spending more but are getting less and less."
2. *Release schedules slip.* "Commitments are made to customers and prospects. Those customers or potential customers are preparing major business initiatives that depend on our release schedule. They need our release, with the functionality we promised, at the exact point in time we promised to deliver it. We usually let them down at the last moment. Their plans are thrown

into disarray, and they lose money and credibility with their customers. We may not get more business from them; they will obviously not act as good references for us; and they may start looking for other vendors."

3. *Stabilization at end of the release takes longer and longer.* "We got really firm with the development organization. We set firm, inflexible dates that they had to be done by. They met these dates by the end of what they call 'code complete' or a 'code freeze.' But the software was unusable. It didn't do what was needed, it didn't perform as required, and it did all of that badly. We couldn't even ship it as a 'beta release' so we could get feedback from a small sample of customers. The defects were so profound that our beta customers refused to participate. We needed another nine months to ship the release, and even then it was shaky and required a lot of hand-holding and apologies."

4. *Planning takes too long and doesn't get it right.* "We figured the releases were taking too long and then slipping because we didn't plan well enough at the start of the work. We didn't get our requirements firmed up and fully developed, and our estimates included more guesses than they should have. To rectify this, we now spend more time planning. New ideas keep coming up. As people review the plans, they find parts that need to be reworked or clarified. We are now spending much more time planning than we used to, but our schedule slips and stabilization periods are still extensive and awful. Despite our significant efforts, changes still come up during development that weren't and couldn't be foreseen during planning."

5. *Changes are hard to introduce mid-release.* "The current process cannot accommodate change. We spent a lot of time planning everything at the beginning, and all the needed work is predicated on the plan. But often something critical has to be included, or a new feature has to be added to close a sale. To incorporate this change, we have to adjust all the work that we have already done to accommodate it. This is very difficult because it is hard to understand the ripple effects of changes in software. Even when it is important, it feels like the amount of time that it takes to fit it in is often a hundred times greater than if we had known of it when we started. But what can we do? If the change doesn't make it into this project or release, it may have to wait up to two more years to be included in the next release."

6. *Quality is deteriorating.* "We know that we shouldn't pressure the developers to get what was planned and changed out on time, but our business is

hurting from the planning, slippage, and change problems. We tell the developers to toughen up and get it out on schedule with everything we planned. Every time we do that the developers accommodate us by cutting the quality of the software or the testing of its suitability. The result is so bad that we either go back into the stabilization phase or we ship an organizational embarrassment."

7. *Death marches are hurting morale*. "We are treating people in a way we would like not to. However, we have commitments and a business to run, so everyone on the project works weekends and long days. Their families and their health suffer. As a consequence, we have trouble recruiting top developers and we lose our best developers to other organizations. Our existing staff is so demoralized that its productivity is slipping despite the increase in hours."

These examples are enough to discourage any executive or manager. Despite 20 years of herculean efforts and massive expenditures in software, by the early 1990s little progress had been made in ensuring the successful outcome of software projects. The process we will describe to you in this book tackles these problems head on.

The Wrong Results: Project Failure

Your use of the traditional, or predictive, software development process is the root cause underlying so many software project failures. The predictive process, also called waterfall, depends on the accuracy of the project plan and its unswerving execution. It depends on:

1. *Requirements* not changing and being completely understood. Any changes in requirements would change the plan, requiring alterations to the plan that create massive ripple effects and frequently rendering already completed work useless. Unfortunately, more than 35 percent of all requirements change during a typical software project. Business customers struggle to fully define these requirements, but the ever-changing marketplace, their incomplete understanding of what they need, and the difficulty of fully describing the anticipated system until it is done make requirement changes inevitable.

2. *Technology* working without any problems. All of the technology the software uses has to perform reliably and as initially planned. Unfortunately,

the project frequently incorporates technologies planners haven't used in the past—either singularly or in combination, or for the same purposes. What's more, technology standards sometimes change during the course of the project.

3. *People* being as predictable and reliable as machines. The plan calls for a specific network of tasks to be completed, each task requiring a defined number of hours from a specifically skilled resource that is given specific well-defined inputs. Unfortunately, the network of tasks starts wobbling whenever requirements change. Even more problematic, people are not machines! People have their good and bad days, different skill levels, and different attitudes and intelligence. Tasks ended up being executed in a very different way than predicted.

The software development industry understands these difficulties and for years has tried to address them by stepping up its planning efforts. Project planning could take as long as the actual development of the software. Massive amounts of work went into gathering requirements, defining architecture, and detailing work plans.

But all of that work was useful only if the plan was based on accurate information that did not change over time. This method is effective when work is well understood and relatively stable and the plan can consequently remain unchanged. When this is not the case, however, the predictive process fails. It is not constructed to cope with the unknown and the unexpected; it is constructed to optimize problems of constraint.

Many traditional manufacturers successfully employ the predictive process model. The payoff for all this upfront work is the repeated execution of the plan, creating car after car or toaster after toaster. There is no similar payoff in software, as a software development plan is executed only once. The very thing that made predictive processes suitable for manufacturing, where a single process cycle will create high volumes of products, make it ill suited for software, where a single process cycle will create just one product.

The Stacey Graph is a useful tool for assessing the certainty or predictability of work.[2] The Stacey Graph measures the certainty versus the unpredictability of various dimensions of work and categorizes where the work

---

[2] R. Stacey, *Complexity and Emergence in Organizations* (London: Routledge, 2001).

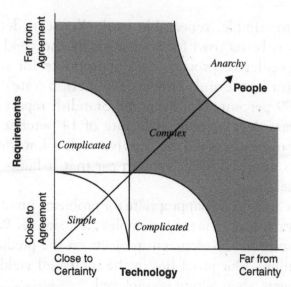

Figure 1.3 The Stacey Graph

falls. We used it to model the three dimensions of software development: requirements, technology, and people, as described in Figure 1.3.

We can plot software development projects as follows:

- *Requirements:* Close to certain with no risk of change, to far from certain, with vague, emergent descriptions and many expected changes.
- *Technology:* Well known and understood, to far from certain, with development and operational technology usually consisting of multiple products interacting through interfaces at different levels of software development and release.
- *People:* Known and constant, with a small number of people on a single team, to software projects involving more than four or five people, often hundreds, who are constantly changing. People by themselves have opinions, attitudes, and moods. Working in groups or teams, the interactions and unpredictability of their work is significant.

Using the Stacey Graph, we can see that software development projects are at least complex and sometimes chaotic. The predictive process, on which waterfall and traditional software development is based, is applicable only for simple, repeatable work. You can determine whether the right process is being used for your work by the yield rate, the degree of success. If a predictive process were appropriate for software projects, the yield rate (or successful project completion rate) would be very high—about 99.99 percent. However, the Standish report discussed earlier measures a software development yield rate of 14 percent using predictive processes. Most businesses could not survive such a low yield rate. Imagine if General Motors scrapped every seventh car that it built—that's the effect of a 14 percent yield rate.

The predictive process is inappropriate for problems involving software development. Software development is complex, not simple. We assert that the decision to base software development projects on the predictive process was what led us to failure. Our proof lies in the increased yield rate of software development projects when Scrum is employed.

People sometimes equate construction or bridge building with software development. Engineering disciplines, such as bridge construction, fall somewhere between simple and complex on the Stacey Graph. Standardization renders this work only complicated. There are three forms of standardization. Firstly, there are Newtonian laws explaining how physical objects interact. Secondly, standardized materials such as wood beams, metal struts, and fasteners, with standard sizes and known characteristics are employed.. Thirdly, there are standards for all types of construction that are written into codes and inspected for by authorities. None of these things exists in software; what's more, as long as the software industry continues to evolve as rapidly as it has, this is unlikely to change.

Case Study: Parametric Technology Corporation

Parametric Technology Corporation (PTC) is a global firm with 5,000 employees that develops product life cycle management products. These products, which grew out of CAD/CAM (computer-aided design/computer-aided manufacturing) systems, help some of the world's largest engineering organizations—Raytheon, BAE Systems, and Airbus, to name a few—to manage the development of massive systems such as the Airbus A380. They do so this in part by tracking the configuration of all the parts, assemblies, and subassemblies.

In 2005, PTC was suffering from all of the symptoms of predictive software development processes:

1. *Releases took longer and longer.* Releases had crept from 18 months to 24 months, and it looked like the current release was going to take longer.
2. *Release schedules were slipping.* Slips from the initial schedule were up to nine months, and these occurred bit by bit. Customers that relied on the timely delivery of critical functionality were unhappy.
3. *Stabilization at end of the release took longer and longer.* Stabilization was behind at least two-thirds of the slips.
4. *Planning took too long and didn't get it right.* Up to six months was spent planning each release, and even then the plan was wrong and would often have to be changed.
5. *Changes were hard to introduce mid-release.* It was hard to tell if the slips, stabilization, and quality problems were due to changes once the project started, but there were certainly a lot of necessary changes.
6. *Quality was deteriorating.* This was both a serious and increasing problem.
7. *Death marches were hurting morale.* PTC was having trouble recruiting quality people.

PTC's development organization employed a waterfall process, and to make it work better, they had tried to button down on requirements. Requirements were compiled into an exhaustive functional specification document. Only when the requirements were finalized were they shared with the development organization. In the meantime, the developers didn't have much to do. They either fixed bugs or sometimes left PTC out of pure boredom. The quality staff wasn't allowed to start any testing until the product was fully complete, so it had less time to do its work. Working under release date pressure, the quality team was forced to release products with insufficient testing.

Jane Wachutka was the new vice president for product development of PTC's Windchill product. As a new employee, she tried the PTC way of waterfall, and she found that all of the usual problems occurred. At her previous job, she had employed many nonwaterfall techniques similar to those that helped the FBI succeed with the Sentinel project. With this approach, a project consists of one or more iterations of work, each no more than 30 days long. Many small teams of developers selected high-value requirements each iteration and turned them into an increment of usable software. All the increments of the teams were integrated into one complete and usable increment. In each subsequent iteration, another increment of software was developed and added to the prior increments.

Brian Shepherd, PTC's executive vice president for product development, was skeptical when Jane advocated this new process for building the software in 2007. If he allowed her to do so, she committed to being able to get the programmers started sooner, improving programmer retention rates, engaging the quality group sooner, and not releasing products until they were fully tested and of sufficient quality. Jane stressed that the functional specifications could be imperfect because the product management group would get to see and use parts of the product frequently during the development cycle and give feedback. Brian agreed to proceed with a new process—an agile process called Scrum. He warned Jane, though, "Don't screw it up."

When Jane first told her employees about the new way they were going to develop software, they were skeptical. The individual members of the development teams, in particular, were slow to buy into it. They still struggled to be perfect at each step of development, making sure they were doing exactly what others wanted. However, as they gained some experience in using the new process, the product managers no longer struggled to complete perfect functional specifications before handoff to development; they let the functional specifications emerge throughout the release. Because PTC now developed complete functionality within 30 days, its developers were able to directly collaborate with customers within any appropriate iteration of development. The developers gained insights into the requirements and how they could be best implemented. Customers noticed the differences and began working with development teams during each iteration. The proud customers helped author the functionality and got exactly what they wanted.

The product management team had a rolling three-, two-, and one-year set of requirements. Three years out was the vision, with a description of high-level capabilities. A more detailed picture of which releases would deliver the vision was available for the two-year time frame. For the current year, 30-day iterations were defined for most of the first six months, and there was a road map of goals for the next six months. Each year's set of requirements had more detail than its predecessor. The developers worked on the one-year set of requirements. They called and worked with PTC customers to work out the details. The entire organization had become a think tank of creativity and productivity.

Within two years, all of Jane's commitments to Brian had been met. Jane's organization was releasing software every 12 months, down from previous release times that exceeded 24 months. The product was of high quality. By 2011, PTC had changed. It had become a transparent organization, both within and to its customers. Surprises rarely happened; customers knew what to expect and when. Defects were low and trending to zero by 2012. New features, user interfaces, and workflow capabilities had been added. The product had been overhauled to make it secure from external threats. Finally, the budget and staffing were both down by more than 10 percent. Brian Shepherd had a new facility built for the software product organization. The space reflected the transparency critical to the new process: Everyone was in an open space, with no offices. All walls were glass.

Recently, Jim Heppelmann, the chief executive officer (CEO) of PTC, listened as his managers positioned themselves for increases in their annual budgets. Finally, he stopped the discussion and asked everyone to thank Jane's organization for reducing costs while improving quality and increasing functionality. Because of them, he said, he could share the savings with others parts of the organization.

In one instance, Jane and Jim were on a conference call to a company in Israel that was evaluating PTC's products. Jane told the CEO that Raytheon was using PTC's products worldwide and she urged him to contact Raytheon's executives. She knew that they were not only impressed with PTC's products; they were thrilled that PTC's new process removed surprises. They were able to collaborate and adjust their schedules in real time with PTC. They were so impressed that they were adopting PTC's way of developing software. Jim jumped in. He told the prospect that Jane had forgotten to mention the last release. It was the best-looking product PTC had ever shipped, primarily because Jane had changed the process.

Summary

Software development has in the past been prone to failure. The root cause of this failure is the use of predictive processes for complex work. When we shift to Scrum, an empirical process, the software project success rate increases dramatically.

It *is* possible to get software features ready to use in 30 days—or less. Don't let your developers tell you otherwise, because hundreds of thousands of software developers have been doing this since the early 2000s. A software product may still be big, but it can still be built in small pieces, one by one, 30 days at a time.

2

Scrum: The Right Process Produces the Right Results

IN THE LAST chapter, we found that an empirical process is the correct process for software development. Now, let's see how empiricism works and how we can develop software using it. We'll explore empiricism through the lens of the agile software development process we have developed over the years, which is called Scrum.

Empiricism in Action

In an empirical process, information is gained by observation, rather than prediction. We also know empirical processes are best for complex problems, where there is more that we do not know than we do know. The two requirements in those situations, for an empirical process to work, are the following:

1. *Inspection and adaptation:* We must frequently inspect where we are so that we can adapt our next steps to optimize the results. The frequency of the inspection and adaptation depends on how much risk we want to take. The greater the unknown, the more quickly we can go off target. The more we go off target, the greater the waste to reorient us, undo the useless work, and start again.

2. *Transparency:* When we make an inspection, we must be able to assess what we are seeing in the same terms as our goal. If our goal is to develop a system with some features and functionality, then we have to inspect something that is a feature, function, or a discrete subset of either.

If we were using a predictive process, we would lay out the requirements for software that might take years to develop. But we know that with software, too much risk can accrue during such a long time period and too much waste is involved if we plan for a project of such long duration. Instead, we use a shorter frequency, typically 30 days or less. (We'll discuss later on the value of shorter frequency.) At the end of the first 30 days, we inspect the results and determine what we should do next to achieve our vision, adapting our course as necessary.

Before we start developing software, we need to have an idea, a vision of some way in which we can create value with software. We think we know how to run an operation more effectively, or we think we know how to create software that others will find valuable. We can describe some aspects of what the software needs to do and the requirements that it must satisfy very clearly. Many other aspects of the software are less clear, and we can leave them undefined until later. What we know ranges from the critically important and well understood to the possibly relevant and only vaguely understood.

We create a list of our ideas, which we call a backlog of requirements (Figure 2.1). We order the product backlog of work so that the most critical requirements are at the top of the list. The backlog is an ever-changing list of our ideas for this software; we can add, modify, or delete items from it whenever we want.

First, we need to ascertain whether our idea is workable. Can we develop something within 30 days (or less) that is useful and justifies further work on the software?

We meet with a small team of software developers. We share our vision and initial requirements with them. We collaborate with them and flesh out the most important requirements. Although the entire system may be extensive, we only focus on just enough to see what is possible and if we want to proceed. We'd also like to get a first look at a usable part of our vision.

We ask the development team how many of the requirements it thinks it can turn into working, completed functionality within the upcoming 30 days.

Partial Product Backlog for Bank						
Line of Business	Operation	Product	Activity	Product Backlog Item	Prty	Size
Trust	....					
Corporate Banking	....					
Consumer Banking	Teller	Mortgage				
		Savings	Deposits	Customer can make a deposit across accounts	33	13
				Customer can perform deposit themselves using new automated teller terminal	42	21
			Withdrawals			
		Checking				
	Platform	IRA	Filing Status			
		401K	Personal Information			
		Mortgage	Location			
		Personal Loan				
		Savings				
		Checking				

Figure 2.1   Backlog of Requirements Organized by Business Operation

We start with the most important items first, but the team may have ideas that need to be included, such as software stability. We talk about these requirements and then help the development team think through the best way to develop them. Although we aren't software developers like the team members, we can choose between alternatives and clarify matters for them.

Let's create some definitions for what we have described:

- *Iteration*. Iterating is the act of repeating a series of steps or a process, usually with the aim of approaching a desired goal or result. Each repetition of the process is also called an iteration, and the results of one iteration are used as the starting point for the next. For you, the first 30 days is the first iteration.
- *Frequency*. This refers to the length of the iteration. Frequent iterations control risks by continually inspecting progress to ensure that waste doesn't occur and control is maintained. Optimal frequency is never less than a week or more than a month.
- *Increment*. An increment is a piece of the whole that increases over time. The functional result of an iteration of the development process is called

an increment. Increments build up, iteration by iteration, until we have a valuable system.

- *Transparency.* The increment must be completely done and usable, with no work remaining. Incomplete work or prototypes are opaque because we have no idea how complete they are and how much work remains to complete them.
- *Iterative incremental.* This is a way of developing software through a sequence of iterations, each of which generates a complete increment of functionality that builds on all previous increments. Iterations continue until a goal is reached and value is optimized.

We start the first iteration. The development team turns our requirements into an increment of functionality. Each iteration starts with planning, then the team develops what was planned, and then everyone inspects the resulting increment of software.

To develop a system that meets our needs and vision, there may be a few or numerous iterations. Each iteration is time boxed; that is, we always allocate and use the complete iteration without changing its length. Each iteration creates an increment of potentially usable software (Figure 2.2). The functionality is complete, with no work left undone. The result of one iteration is used as the starting point for the next iteration.

At the end of each iteration, we can direct the development team to go in a different direction from what we may have initially conceived. In fact, the likelihood of this happening is high. Initially, we have a vision or an opportunity that we want to take advantage of. We have a development team create a software application that addresses a highly important aspect of this. We look at the increment. Then we start thinking about how we will use it. We start

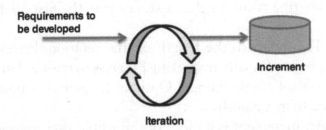

Requirements to be developed

Increment

Iteration

Figure 2.2 One Iteration Produces One Transparent Increment

thinking about what we could add to the increment to make it more useful. In some disciplines, this is referred to as mid-course correction. It occurs with each iteration.

Each increment we have developed while in pursuit of our vision spurs us to think of more creative or specific ways to realize the vision. It may provoke a dialog between the development team and us. We might collaborate about how we can get the most value from the next iteration and what we want done in it. We can embrace change.

We may find that our vision is not realistic. The technology may not be ready for prime time, we may not like the results, or we may find that the cost will be too high. Depending on our finding, we may stop at this point. We spend no more money until we find a more feasible vision. Successful projects include those that do not waste money.

Sometimes one iteration is enough to develop something we can start using while we direct the development team to develop more functionality. We can build more capabilities and functionality, iteration by iteration, as we take advantage of the opportunity more fully. Each increment piggybacks on the previous ones. When the result of the development team's work is deemed right, we release the software for people to start using. Figure 2.3 illustrates several iterations.

We have devised an empirical process for software development. We make decisions about what to do next at the end of each iteration, always keeping

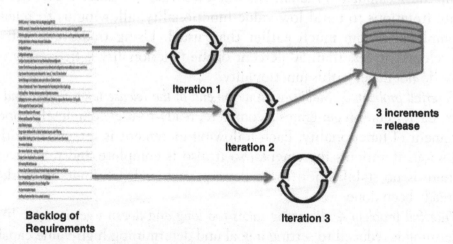

Figure 2.3 Several Iterations Generate an Increment of Additive Functionality

our vision in mind. We review what was developed. We can extrapolate the probable cost and delivery date to see if we want to proceed. We call this an iterative incremental process. It is a foundation of the Scrum process. We have described how it works and why it might be called software in 30 days. Now let's see if this process solves the problems that we found with the waterfall, or predictive, process. Let's see if this process solves those and even other problems.

Does Empiricism Resolve Our Problems?

Does our empirical solution solve the waterfall problems? Let's evaluate it against the pain points we observed in waterfall:

- *Waterfall problem 1: Releases take longer and longer.* Our releases will consist of a stack of integrated increments, developed sequentially, iteration after iteration. We can stop iterating whenever we want. We can stop when we have maximized our value, especially since we found that more than half of software is rarely or never used. We can also just stop and release when a date or budget is reached. We will have accumulated valuable increments to implement.
- *Waterfall problem 2: Release schedules slip.* Our release schedule cannot slip more than 30 days, since that is the maximum length of one iteration. We ship the accumulated increments when we reach the date. We do not allocate iterations to build low-value functionality, allowing us to release a completed system much earlier than usual. Using traditional software development, less than 50 percent of the functionality is frequently used. We do not develop this functionality.
- *Waterfall problem 3: Stabilization at the end of the release takes longer and longer.* Each iteration generates a complete, ready-to-use, completely done increment of functionality. Each following increment is integrated with all previous iteration's increments, so it also is complete and ready to use. There is no stabilization to be done prior to release since all work has already been done.
- *Waterfall problem 4: Planning takes too long and doesn't get it right.* Initial planning is reduced to setting a goal and determining high-value capabilities, functionality, and features that are needed to reach the goal. The

anticipated date and cost are then forecast. Planning prior to the first iteration is usually 20 percent of what we used to spend for waterfall, or predictive, projects. We plan the requirements for each iteration in detail only immediately prior to starting the iteration. This iteration planning is called just-in-time planning, and the requirements are said to be emergent as we inspect results and adapt the best requirements for the next iteration.

- *Waterfall problem 5: Changes are hard to introduce mid-release.* There is no mid-release in an incremental iterative project. Requirements can emerge and be requested prior to any iteration, with minimal overhead.
- *Waterfall problem 6: Quality is deteriorating.* Every iteration's increment is complete and ready to use. Its quality is already built in. Each subsequent increment is also added with fit-for-purpose quality. There is no rushed stabilization period at the end of a project when quality might be compromised to satisfy a date commitment. The work is already done.
- *Waterfall problem 7: Death marches are hurting morale.* The end of release stabilization has been eliminated, along with the death march of overtime and weekend work that it causes.

As you can see, iterative incremental development based on empirical process control addresses the problems that used to haunt software development. To meet the needs of any organization, though, we have to know how to manage these projects. This is covered next, and in more detail in Chapter 6.

The work can be managed using just three variables. First are (A) requirements, the functionality that will deliver the envisioned software. Second is (B) time, which for now we measure in units of 30 days. Third is (C) work completed, which is measured in usable pieces of functionality delivered, or the amount of (A) done in any 30-day time period, and cumulatively.

You can create a chart to manage the project, as follows:

1. Requirements backlog is on the y-axis, or vertical axis. The effort to meet each requirement is sized. Let's assume we have five requirements. They are 2, 3, 5, 3, and 8 units of effort to do. They create a stack of work on the y-axis that is 21 units of work high. The units are ordered by sequence in which you want them turned into usable functionality. Let's say the order, top down, is 2, 3, 5, 3, and 8 still.

2. Time is on the x-axis, or horizontal axis. The units are 30-day periods of time, the iteration length.
3. We anticipate based on past experience with the development team that they will complete five units of work every iteration. We will find out the team's actual productivity once we start, but this is a forecast based on yesterday's weather. We thus anticipate completing twenty units of work in the first four iterations (5, 5, 5, 5), and the last piece of work in the fifth and last iteration.
4. The amount of work completed and functionality ready to use is calculated at the end of each iteration. We are planning that the first two requirements, which are 2 and 3 units of work, will be completed in the first iteration. We anticipate completing the next piece of functionality, whose size is 5, in the second iteration. By this time, we usually have changed our minds about what to do next. We have seen the first two increments, and we often find unexpected or modified requirements for the next iteration. If not, we proceed as planned. However, the plan and upcoming requirements may change without penalty at the end of any iteration. Increments' size is measured in the same units as the requirements on the y-axis.
5. The development team created 3, 5, and 5 units of functionality in the first three periods of time. The resulting chart is shown in Figure 2.4.

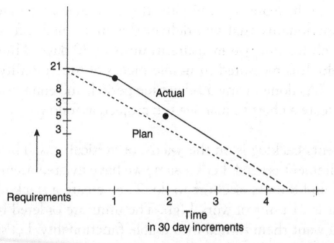

Figure 2.4 Work Burndown

The plan, or forecast, at the start of the work shows you starting with 21 units of work. Five are anticipated to be completed every iteration. We plot that accordingly. The forecast line on the chart plans all functionality to be complete and ready to use soon in the fifth iteration.

The actual requirements completed show 3 units of work done in the first iteration, with 5, and 5 more units of work completed in the second and third itererations. We plotted this progress above on the actual plot line. If we create a trend line from this work, it appears that all work will be complete by the middle, not the start, of the fifth iteration. However, that is a projection, not a certainty. Empiricism means that we will not be sure of how much work can be done until it is done. In the first iteration we had anticipated 5 units of work. Only 3 were done. The technology was shakier than anticipated, one of our requirements wasn't clear, and one of the developers was sick for several days. We inspected our progress at the end of the first iteration. We decided that the return on investment was still good. We felt that the problems in the first iteration probably weren't going to recur. Based on these calculations, we risked funding another iteration. This inspection and adaptation occurs at the end of each iteration.

Empiricism supports the following:

1. *Management:* You know exactly how many and which requirements you have completed and which are ready for use at the end of each iteration. You can make future projections based on past progress and assess the probable completion date. You make the projection knowing that this may change at the end of the next iteration.
2. *Control:* If the information reflects completion later than desired, you can reduce the size or amount of remaining functionality to be done. For instance, at the end of the second iteration, with 13 units of requirements still to be done, you could have reduced the scope of the remaining requirements to 10 units. If the development team continued with 5 units of requirements in each of the next two iterations, the functionality would be complete at the end of the fourth iteration.
3. *Predictability:* The forecast could be wrong. Completion would be several weeks later than anticipated. The likelihood of this happening could be suspected after the first iteration, made probable after the second iteration, and made most likely by the end of the third iteration. Everyone who was

going to use the functionality could have started adjusting his or her schedule in synch. Similarly, the budget could have been revised and approved early.

4. *Risk management:* The development team completed only 2 units of functionality in each of the first three iterations. At the end of the third iteration, a forecast would indicate that completion wouldn't occur until the middle of the tenth iteration. If the initial budget had been $100,000, the new forecast would have predicted an overrun of $150,000. If the return on the investment of $250,000 were inadequate, the project could be cancelled after the third iteration.

People Practices Stemming from Empiricism

Because the empirical approach provides visibility into what works and what doesn't work, we rapidly learned and codified a set of best practices for this style of development. These practices came in part from principles in academia, but they also came from the on-the-ground practice of teams in action.

Overall, we have found that small teams of software developers best perform iterative incremental work. Teams typically should consist of no more than nine people and no fewer than three people. Together, the team must have all the skills necessary to turn your requirements into increment of functionality that realize your vision. Depending on the type of software the software developers are building, the developers on the team should have skills that include programming, testing, design, analysis, documentation, architecture, or more. The team attributes we want to engender through team structure, practices, and norms are productivity, quality, creativity, and continuous improvement.

Our insights into the most effective software teams draw heavily on the work of Takeuchi and Nonaka, who studied the team process at Harvard University.[1] They observed the behaviors of autonomous teams motivated by a higher purpose, engaged in cross learning, and working in short iterations. The intense collaboration of these teams facilitated a knowledge generation cycle that led to innovation, faster time to market, and higher quality. The

[1] H. Takeuchi and I. Nonaka, "The New New Product Development Game," *Harvard Business Review* (Jan–Feb 1986).

teams reminded them of the game of rugby, so they called this style of project management Scrum, for when the game is restarted after the ball has gone out of play.

Based on our learning from Takeuchi and Nonaka, we developed the following people practices to complement the structure of an empirical software development process. These practices all lead to high-performance teams that exhibit creativity, quality, productivity, and morale:

- *Respect for the individual worker*: In some companies workers are treated like children, their ideas diminished, and told what to do every moment of the day. In order for people to be excited and engaged with their work, their environment has to be one of encouragement and respect. Scrum is designed to ensure that workers are treated with respect and admiration. We were not the first to think of the ideas and practices used in Scrum. Most are industry best practices. However, Jeff really focused on the "people" aspect of software development in the Scrum environment.
- *Built-in instability*: The development process begins with top management setting aggressive, broad goals or strategic direction. It does not hand off a clear product or work plan but gives the development team a wide measure of freedom. Setting challenging requirements creates a dynamic tension within the team.
- *Self-organizing project teams*: The team itself decides how to meet management's demanding goals. The idea is to force the team not to rely on outside guidance, but to organize and manage itself. Self-organization is evident when the team exhibits three conditions: autonomy, self-transcendence, and cross-fertilization. Autonomy is there because management is limited to providing guidance, money, and support. It seldom intervenes. In a way, management acts like a venture capitalist; they open their purses and keep their mouths shut. Teams constantly strive to do things better. It is an unending search for the limit of performance.
- *Cross-fertilization*: Colocated, cross-functional teams foster high performance, quality, and creativity. Team members work collaboratively, and the lines between specialties start to blur. In fact, some companies mandate that every team member have two specialties (for example, coding in more than one language and testing) and two domains (for example, design and marketing). The intense interaction of the individuals begins to develop a

pulse or tempo for the team. The heartbeat of innovation and performance emerges.

- *Overlapping development phases:* By avoiding linear sequencing of work, the team is able to absorb the "vibration" or "noise" generated by blocks in the development process. When a bottleneck appears, the team does not come to a sudden halt; it works around the problem. Overlapping phases do away with the traditional notion of division of labor. Not only does this approach yield speed and flexibility, but the shared responsibility and cooperation stimulate involvement and commitment, as well as sensitivity to market conditions. The downside is managing an intensive process that requires visibility, communication, tension, and even conflict.

- *Multilevel and multifunctional learning:* Learning in the team takes on multiple dimensions. At 3M, for example, engineers are encouraged to use 15 percent of their company time to pursue their dreams. If a team is blocked at Honda, its members may be sent to Europe to "look around and see what is happening there." The idea is that learning often takes place in non-obvious ways and places, and most importantly, it comes from personal initiative fostered and guided by management.

- *Subtle control:* Although project development teams are on their own, they are not uncontrolled. The emphasis is on self-control, and enough checkpoints are established to prevent instability, ambiguity, and tension from turning into chaos. Control through peer pressure and "control by love" are the basis of subtle control. The dynamic flow of the team surfaces the tacit (unconscious) knowledge of the group and creates explicit knowledge in the form of software. This dynamic flow emerges only in an environment of caring created by management. Team leaders are carefully selected, and teams are balanced by changing people to help introduce the right dynamic and ensure that people get along and can work together. There needs to be a set of shared values. Incentives need to be team based. Mistakes are anticipated and tolerated.

- *Transfer of learning:* Knowledge generation within the team is not enough to be successful in the market. That hard-won knowledge needs to be shared throughout the company. A company may seed new teams with experienced people. Project activities discovered at work are moved across the company as standard practices. At the same time, unlearning is as important as learning. The market changes quickly, and old ways may no longer work. Management makes new demands that clearly cannot be met by old ways of doing things.

We have found that the following practices also enhance software development:

- *People:* People are most productive when they manage themselves. People take their commitment more seriously than other people's commitment for them. People have many creative moments during downtime. People always do the best they can. And under pressure to work harder, people automatically and increasingly reduce quality.
- *People in teams:* Teams and people do their best work when they aren't interrupted. Teams improve most when they solve their own problems. And broadband, face-to-face communication is the most productive way for teams to work together.
- *Team composition:* Teams are more productive than the same number of individuals. Products are more robust when a team has all of the cross-functional skills focused on the work. Changes in team composition often lower productivity for a time.

Even When We Know Better

Although the predictive, or waterfall, process is in trouble, many people and organizations continue to try to make it work. We met the chief technology officer (CTO) of Marks and Spencer, a UK retailer, and his staff in 2005 to discuss empiricism and Scrum. He had just upgraded his entire development organizations process, acquiring the entire suite of methodologies, tools, training, and implementation services from PricewaterhouseCoopers (PWC), an international consultancy. The PWC approach was predictive, or waterfall.

But he was curious and wanted to understand empiricism. It sounded familiar. As we explained the process to him, he became visibly excited. He broke in to tell us that his organization used empiricism. Whenever one of their large development projects, using the PWC approach, got in trouble, they would halt. They would then use this approach to get it back on track, or sometimes even to finish it. He said this was their "ace in the hole," meaning their trick that would get them out of tough spots.

We asked him what he did after the empirical approach got him out of the hole. Without considering the irony, he told us that they then went back to using the approved PWC approach. Knowing how to do things didn't mean that they were allowed to do so unless it was an emergency.

Agility

As our world becomes more complex, there are many more opportunities for businesses and organizations. The dream of every entrepreneur and business-person with an entrepreneur's heart is to take advantage of an opportunity—to find out what is possible, what the costs might be, and what risks are to anticipate. When risks are tolerable, entrepreneurs want to proceed step by step, as fast as they can go, to capture opportunities. However, as much as we want to control risks, things quickly can get out of control. Daring caution or cautious daring is desirable. We termed the ability to take advantage of opportunities *agility*. Agility is a measure of one's ability to successfully take advantage of an opportunity. We can turn on a dime, immediately launch bold initiatives, and manage our risks. We can make our competitors weep when they wake up in the morning, and we can please our newly found customers.

Agility is the ability to take advantage of opportunities or to rise to meet challenges with calculated risk. It is the most significant competitive advantage today. We create this advantage and control our risks by limiting all our projects to 30 days or less.

In this way, we get to try ideas without regretting pursuing them. We know early on if they are too costly, unrealistic, or impossible, and we stop them before more money is spent.

Summary

We need to be able to take advantage of opportunities and respond effectively to challenges. We need to be able to explore many ideas, change our minds, and let the best solution emerge. If you see an opportunity or want to mount an initiative, you can not only achieve your goals but also hone them in order to deliver only the most valuable functionality. With more control and a faster, less risky process, you can get something off the ground within 30 days and continue to improve it.

Empirical software development, employing iterative incremental practices, has been around for more than 20 years. Using it, you can create tight control over risk with time-limited increments of software. It provides transparency through the delivery of complete increments of business functionality every 30 days (or less) so that waste can be eliminated. It creates the agility or flexibility to tweak the application to better meet emerging requirements and thereby increases applicability significantly. We no longer worry about the progress of our software development work. We no longer worry about meeting our commitments. We no longer worry about having to ask for increased budgets. We no longer have to depend on abstractions of progress, such as Gantt charts and prototypes. We know exactly where we are in terms of value and schedule at least every 30 days.

3

Try It Yourself: The Pilot

IF YOU ARE still interested, it is now appropriate to see if empirical software development solves your problems and meets your needs. This is the time to conduct a pilot—a small-scale preliminary study—to evaluate feasibility, time, and costs and to uncover adverse effects. In this chapter we tell you:

1. How to run a pilot study of this new approach to software development.
2. What information you can gain from this pilot.
3. How this has worked for others who have done it (the issues they discovered and what they needed to address).

You are critical. In this chapter we describe to you what you need to do to help this succeed, step by step. We also provide a more thorough description and some examples; these can be read later when the pilot is under way.

The process followed during the pilot is quite simple:

1. Form the team.
2. Figure out what you want to pilot.
3. Do a small piece of it, completely.
4. Evaluate what you want to do next.
5. Assess what can be improved and do it.
6. Continue iterating Steps 3 through 5 until satisfied.

Before starting, figure out what will happen if the pilot fails or succeeds. How much time and money are you willing to spend on something that isn't working for you before giving up? What will you do if valuable functionality is delivered, increment by increment, and you want to proceed? By the end of the pilot, you will know if you want to engage in empirical software development on a larger scale. Of course, you will also have the software that was developed during the pilot.

Empiricism Is Used Elsewhere in the Organization

Another thing to do before starting is to realize that, most likely, the empirical process is already rooted in other parts of the organization. It will seem new only for software development. For example, a typical sales organization employs empiricism throughout its yearly cycle. First it establishes an annual plan. The anticipated sales for the year are projected. A pipeline of accounts and customers is projected, showing the sources of the sales revenues. For the first several months of the year, the prospects are well known and the steps to conclude the sales are specific. Prospects that are known and likely to buy are included in projections for the second quarter. Ideas, contacts, and reasons for purchases are identified. Projections for the last half of the year are vague and include ideas, targets of opportunities, and renewals.

As the year progresses, sales managers continually update the pipeline. Likely revenues are identified for two or three months into the future, and the plan remains vague for the rest of the year. Every month, sales, changes in upcoming sales, and the forecast are reviewed. Future sales efforts and company expenditures are adjusted accordingly. The process is as follows:

1. *Form the team.* Bring the sales force together, discuss how the company is doing, review the competitive landscape, and inform salespeople of any new products.
2. *Figure out what you want to do.* Project the sales pipeline, targets, and revenues for the year with decreasing precision. Assign territories and quotas.
3. *Do a small piece of it, completely.* Sell for a month and see what happens. Also see what happens to the pipeline for the future.
4. *Evaluate what you want to do next.* Update the pipeline and refocus the efforts for the upcoming month.
5. *Continue doing and evaluating.* Repeat these steps each month.

A sales organization would never consider using a predictive process. Too little is known and too much will change to plan a year's revenues and sources on the first day of the year.

An Example Pilot to Model

As we stated earlier, a pilot study is a small-scale preliminary study conducted to evaluate feasibility, time, costs, and adverse events. Its purpose is to determine whether you think empirical processes will help you with your software development. We suggest that you try the pilot on something that has presented you with serious problems. It should be something that is tricky, that is difficult, or that you aren't sure about.

The following example of a pilot project may serve as a model for one that you conduct. An Ohio-based financial organization has many mutual funds for different sectors and customers. Most of its customers manage their own accounts through an online portal. A vice president (VP) in the mutual fund division had a smartphone and had been using some of the applications, such as one for paying bills. He wondered if an app that would let people do most of their fund management on their smartphones would be useful for his customers. He thought that such an app might generate more activity from current customers. If it could be announced and delivered before the competition developed one, the app might even attract more customers.

He took this idea to the information technology (IT) people and asked for their help. They liked the idea and were interested in exploring it; they had wanted to expand into mobile technologies. The IT team proposed that they start by developing the requirements for the app. They estimated that this would take five or six months. When the requirements were known, they would be able to commit to a cost and schedule. Five analysts and a project manager would develop the requirements.

The VP needed to fund this first phase of the project with $500,000—a lot of money for just requirements describing what he wanted. The cost of developing the software was still unknown but would probably be multiples of the initial cost. For this type of expenditure, he would have to submit proposals to his boss, the capital committee, and IT (for scheduling). Nobody was going to risk that much money without being convinced that the idea would pay off.

A pilot would determine whether this was a cost-justifiable venture. Using empirical software development, the VP could determine this quickly. He also could create the most important part of the app during the pilot. He estimated that he needed only three iterations of software development. He would engage three software developers, with a budget of $125,000.

To obtain approval for his pilot, he prepared a presentation. He went to his boss, the managers for his division, and the IT steering committees. He discussed with them what he wanted to do, using the presentation. The first slide identified the purpose of the pilot: to determine whether this smartphone app was a good investment for the organization. He showed how the application was aligned with the organization's business strategies. He briefly explained the empirical approach to software development—how it works and why he wanted to try it. He explained that it was not antithetical to the organization's technology strategies. He then described the rest of the project. He said that one result of the pilot could be a working app that could be developed further. The full cost of the app could be extrapolated from the data of the three-month pilot. The VP and the organization would also learn whether empirical software development worked in the organization.

He adjusted his plan to meet their objections. One modification was that he added an IT project manager who had previous experience with iterative, incremental, software development. That increased his budget to $170,000, but it would help the IT department evaluate empirical software development. The IT person would be the pilot manager. If he had any free time, he also could help the team with software testing.

The VP received approval on the condition that the stakeholders from his business unit and IT would be able to review the progress every month with him and his development team.

Form the Team

Once the pilot was approved, his first step was to form the team with the help of the IT pilot manager. Their first decision was that the developers should be from inside the IT organization, not outside contractors. They then assessed who would be appropriate to work on the pilot project. If they recruited people who weren't good developers, they might learn that they couldn't create an increment of software. That would be better than finding this out at the end of a 12-month waterfall project, but it wouldn't achieve the pilot's goals. If they recruited the best developers in the organization, they would find that they could build an increment of software, because the best developers find a way to succeed in any circumstances. So they selected typical developers from the IT organization who met these qualifications:

1. They understood how to develop software using the technology for the pilot.
2. They had, together, all the skills needed to develop a complete piece of software.
3. They had some awareness of iterative incremental development. At least one person on the team had developed software like this and could guide the others.
4. They were volunteers rather than draftees.
5. They were enthusiastic.

The pilot manager helped the VP secure an adequate environment within which to conduct the pilot. Because the developers would be turning his ideas into software, they set up a working space right outside of the VP's operation. The pilot manager also recommended the following:

1. The workspace would be designed so that all team members could easily see and hear one another and work closely with one another. This would allow them to communicate efficiently and to quickly spot and remedy misunderstandings. The workspace would be open, with no dividing walls.
2. Flip charts and whiteboards in the space would help the team members visualize options and explore ideas. The space didn't need to be fancy, but it should be somewhere where team members could leave their stuff throughout the pilot.
3. The team members should work full-time, as part-time team members may not be available when other team members need them. Even when they are available, they may be distracted by other work.
4. Everyone would put in a regular workday. Turning requirements into a usable increment of software requires problem solving. Sending the team members home at the end of a normal workday would allow time for their subconscious minds to take over, positing new approaches and spotting errors.

The VP then formed a team that consisted of him, the pilot manager, and three software developers.

Create a Message That Attracts Team Members

Sometimes it is difficult to attract good software developers. You may have trouble attracting people if they don't understand what's in it for them. Everyone who will be working with the team must understand the purpose and scope of the pilot.

Curaspan Message Discourages Potential Employees Here is an example. Curaspan's online software is used in the hospital community to manage the orderly flow of patient documentation from hospital discharge to rehabilitation or other long-term, posthospitalization facilities. Curaspan was having trouble. Its software was more than 10 years old. Performance was becoming unacceptably slow. Customer service calls were spreading to everyone in the company.

Curaspan hired Edwin Miller as vice president of product management. He had turned around several companies using empirical software development. Curaspan's executives expected him to do the same for them. Edwin began recruiting developers to build the next generation of software. He reached out to the usual suspects: old friends, people who were known in the industry, and recruiting firms. He sifted through resumes and brought the right people in for interviews. Edwin made a number of offers to applicants, but none were accepted.

The problem was that the executives and developers at Curaspan were not convinced that the empirical approach was the right one. They didn't really understand it. Their lack of strategic commitment, their ignorance of the work the people would be doing, and their antipathy toward empirical processes scared the applicants. Even in a bad recession, good developers have other alternatives.

People sense a good thing. Even if you are about to experiment with something you haven't done before, you need to craft a clear message to the people you are going to recruit (internally or externally). Lay out the possibilities and what you will do for them. Describe the risks and the opportunities.

Collocate the Team Members at Iron Mountain Iron Mountain Digital is a $3.1 billion data management company that offers offsite computer data (digital) storage through its LiveVault product. In 2006, the LiveVault product group was struggling. It hadn't released any new software for more than 12 months. Individuals at LiveVault had read about the empirical software development process, Scrum, but were still using old software development practices. Unaware of these difficulties, Iron Mountain's marketing arm had negotiated a contract with Microsoft in June 2007. Microsoft provided software to its customers that backed up their servers regularly. The backup was on a local server, and Microsoft wanted to offer an offsite alternative on LiveVault.

As product manager, Paul Luppino concluded the negotiations with Microsoft to build a new release of LiveVault. The contract stipulated that Microsoft would provide this offsite backup to its customers by February 2008. Iron Mountain asked Paul to take over as program manager for this. The product was to be developed by Iron Mountain developers in Southborough, Massachusetts; Microsoft developers in Bangalore, India; Microsoft product managers in Redmond, Washington; and Paul, in Southborough. It had to be ready in six months.

Paul's back was against the wall, and his job was made more difficult by having teams and an organization that operated out of many locations. Paul had multiple partners, a corporate commitment, a due date, a dispirited development group, and a 12-month history of failure.

Paul had heard about Scrum, so he immediately ordered training for everyone on the project at Iron Mountain. At the same time, he started development iterations. Paul didn't know what his problems were. He knew that if he investigated everything and came up with a plan, months could pass. He figured out that if he started development right away, he would find out what the problems were as he went along. The iterations would let him and Iron Mountain know within 30 days if they were in trouble or if the project was feasible.

Everyone struggled with the physical distance between the participating teams. Video conferencing was expensive, Skype didn't work well enough, and travel was too expensive. Everyone coordinated their work through daily meetings (using very expensive video conferencing, e-mail, and social media tools such as Wikis) that connected Iron Mountain developers in

Massachusetts, Microsoft developers in India, and Microsoft product managers in Washington to help evaluate progress and replan upcoming work. All the managers inspected incremental progress every 30 days. First the people in each location would review the completed increment and then they would teleconference to discuss progress and problems and plan the contents for the next iteration. Training helped everyone become more effectively organized and provided rules of engagement. Paul had the engineering environment at Iron Mountain upgraded so that the developers could be more productive and efficient. Waste from uncoordinated work having to be redone was eliminated. Waste from manual testing when automated testing could be done also was removed. The top management at Iron Mountain became bullish about Live-Vault. New marketing programs and sales efforts were initiated. Three more releases occurred within the next six months.

Figure Out What You Want to Do

Going back to the example of the Ohio-based financial organization, the VP located his development team in an open space near his office. He shared his ideas about the app. He said that he wanted to check out empirical software development to see if it would help rapidly build some software. The team members spent a day getting to know one another. They explored what the app might look like and selected an initial user interface look and "feel." They assessed security, performance, and stability requirements for the app. They wrote down what the app might do when it was completed and what they thought they could do in three monthly iterations.

The team decided that, to determine whether the app was feasible, they needed to find out the following within one iteration (one month):

1. Can the team develop an app with this technology?
2. Can the app connect effectively to the functionality on the portal, bypassing the portal's web user interface?
3. What does this app look like, roughly?

The team members decided what would have to be accomplished—what functionality would have to be achieved—to answer their questions. The minimum goal was to get the log-on screen to appear and reject their user ID. If possible, they wanted to get the log-on to work and open the portal's functionality to the app.

The five people on the team had never worked together closely and had individually never worked on this type of application and technology. They had many ideas and objections. The more they talked, the more they struggled with how to work together. The pressure of having to complete an increment within the iteration added more stress.

A crucial conversation is one that is about something important and around which there are strong feelings. These conversations occur only when everyone feels safe. Everyone needs to feel that he or she will be respected. Everyone should feel safe to argue, to disagree, and to struggle for the best approach. The pilot manager had been through this before. He talked about respect and the need for people to feel safe. He helped the team create some rules of etiquette for close teamwork. These included not putting other's ideas down, not disparaging others, and not calling others negative names. Without these and other rules that emerged, the close work of a team in an open space would have been difficult.

Do a Small Piece of It, Completely

The first order of business was to plan what the software would look like. The next step was to plan how the team would turn the design into working software.

The team decided that they would pause and take stock of how they were doing every day. They would evaluate what had been accomplished and what problems had been encountered. Then they would decide on the most valuable work to do the next day.

Day by day, the team members fitted together the various pieces of the puzzle. They got the app to connect through the smartphone operating system to the portal software. They determined the communication protocols for interactions. They found how to activate the log-on functionality on the portal. The VP and pilot manager reminded them that they also had to show that the app was secure and stable and that it performed well. The team members set up some tests to assess these characteristics and altered the software to meet the requirements.

A side note: Other people in the IT organization had things that they wanted the developers on the team to do. They came to the open area where the team worked and interrupted the team. The pilot manager told them to leave. He told them they would have to solve their problems elsewhere.

Even what appears to be only a few interruptions can reduce the effectiveness of the team by more than 50 percent. The VP knew that he was on the hook to see if empirical software development would work and he wasn't going to blow his and the team's chances through diversions and interruptions.

Evaluate What You Want to Do Next

The team had developed some of the software for the app by the end of the iteration. Anybody could download the app to a smartphone, launch it (which initiated a connection to the portal), and see the same log-on that people using the portal used. The software was stable and met all the requirements. It was well developed and could be readily and safely enhanced. Although the team members had hoped to have more functionality in the log-on, they were pleased with the outcome, as was the VP.

The VP arranged a 4-hour meeting at the end of the iteration to review what had happened. Several other people from the mutual fund division and some of the IT managers also attended the meeting. With their help, the VP and the team evaluated how the empirical process had worked. They discussed the no interruption policy and were convinced of its necessity. They also looked at the design of the app and how it connected to the portal. Several improvements were suggested. The other business managers also had some suggestions about the look and feel of the portal.

Toward the end of the meeting, the pilot manager reminded them that they had to decide whether to proceed with the remaining two iterations. Several people thought that enough had been learned and that the pilot could be therefore be terminated. The fund manger did not agree. He and the majority wanted to proceed. They wanted to see if the empirical software development process would continue to work. They also wanted to further develop the smartphone app.

Several people at the meeting were very critical. They reminded the developers that they had planned get the log-on working but had failed to do so. They told the developers that they were very disappointed. The VP reminded them that this was unknown ground. The team members were experimenting and exploring. They did the best they could during the iteration and gained skill and knowledge.

The discussion then turned to the difference between traditional, or predictive, software development and the empirical process. The VP, backed by the pilot manager, reminded everyone that the point of empiricism is to find out what is possible, what can be done. Once everyone saw the results of an iteration, they could plan the next set of work. He reminded everyone that after just one iteration, he had a piece of working software. Not only that, but he had gained valuable evidence about the feasibility of the app and had something he could start sharing with customers. He had a building block of software that he could keep adding to. If he had done this the predictive way, as he first requested, he would have only documentation of some of his requirements.

The VP decided that he would start showing the app to some of his customers. He would try to determine whether they would actually use the app and how important it would be to them. He would work with customers during each iteration and would include them in the next evaluation so that they could offer their opinions.

Assess What Can Be Improved and Do It

The pilot manger suggested that the team meet to conduct a review—a retrospective of how the iteration had gone. He wanted the team members to openly discuss their feelings and their opinions about how things could be improved. Any of the following could have happened during the iteration and needed to be discussed by the team:

- *Very little functionality was developed.* A development team should always strive to deliver at least one piece of business functionality with every iteration, no matter how small. However, in some cases, the developers may create very little or no usable functionality during the iteration. They may have had to develop a lot of technology, architecture, or automation to get anything done, which subtracts from the time in which they could create functionality. Or they may not be good enough developers to justify the cost and may need to be retrained or replaced.
- *The functionality delivered may not be close enough to what was desired.* The VP may have found that the developers didn't understand what he wanted.

He may have found that he needed to work more closely with the members of the development team to better communicate the vision and requirements and to make sure that they understood them. If they had little knowledge of apps or funds management, he may have to spend more time working with them or find new team members.

- *The iteration felt very awkward.* Pilot team members may feel like people learning a new dance. They may need to examine how they can work together differently—in a way that feels better and gets better results.
- *The team members didn't work together well at all.* The way in which the team members work together may need to be examined. An outside facilitator may be brought in to help them better communicate or make better decisions. Perhaps the team should be reformed with other people. Of course, creating a new team means that the prior experience is lost.

Based on the discussion, the pilot manager asked the team members to suggest several things they would do differently in the upcoming iteration—changes that would improve their work and effectiveness.

Continue Doing and Evaluating Until You Are Finished

A pilot produces one, and sometimes two, valuable things. The first is an assessment of iterative, or incremental, development at your organization. The second may be software that you start using and get value from.

The assessment is not just whether the empirical process works. We already know that it does. The real question is, does it work in your organization? Iteration by iteration evidence mounts to show how well teams work, the productivity that can arise from them, and what they can create of value in a single iteration. Iteration by iteration you also learn how well prepared your organization and its developers are for iterative, or incremental, development. We learn about the skills of our developers. We find out if they possess skills to develop something of value in one iteration. We see if they are able to focus as a team and create something or if the challenge overwhelms them.

You will also see the friction iterative, or incremental, development creates with the rest of the organization. Perhaps the people needed on the team have scarce skills and are needed elsewhere. Sometimes, they team has so many external commitments that they can't work just on the pilot and the overall productivity drops as a result.

Regardless, you often will accumulate, iteration by iteration, software more rapidly than anything you have experienced previously. You may wish to plow through the problems and build something that can be deployed and implemented.

As the iterations complete, you accumulate a picture of the scope and depth of work needed to make iterative, or incremental, development work in your organization. When a waterfall approach was employed, these shortcomings weren't apparent. Their impact on the overall value of software development was hidden. When you employ 30-day development cycles, everything that didn't work under waterfall and that was wasteful becomes transparent. This is good information, but it often spells out the need for a concerted improvement effort. These efforts are detailed in Section 2.

Team Members May Work in Ways That Are New to Them

Self-Organization

In the empirical process, members of a development team figure out how to turn the requirements they are given into usable functionality. No manager tells the team members what to do. The team members collaborate to devise and coordinate their own work plan. They conduct a short meeting every day to replan their work. They can adjust their work daily to optimize results.

Self-organization feels risky. If the time taken for self-organization is too long, team members sometimes don't remain focused on the vision. However, with an iteration of 30 days or less, a team usually stays focused. Remember, you are never risking more than 30 days of work in trying to determine what a team can do.

With predictive software development, plans are created by "experts." Project managers ensure that people do the tasks they are responsible for. People don't have to collaborate and innovate; they just do what they are told to do. When a manager plans the work and ensures that people do what is planned, those people are constrained by the manager's intelligence, vision, organizational skills, and so forth. When they run into problems or unanticipated situations, they are not empowered to think on their own. In the past, they may have been punished for acting on their own, particularly if they failed. So they are not likely to take the risk of innovating.

Self-organization is based on the idea that software developers are capable, intelligent people. They are capable of conducting complex lives outside of the workplace, such as when they drive, have families, shop, and so on. When left on their own within the time-box of an iteration, they act responsibly and do their best. The result is the sum of their intelligence, and the increment emerges from their collaboration.

Here is another example. Sylvain Moussad is vice president of software development at PTC and works directly for Jane Wachutka. His product area employed more than 300 software developers. He initially believed that he and his managers should devise the work for the 50 software development teams. They matched the people to the work and formed the best teams that they could. Yet the teams weren't very productive.

The leaders in the teams told Sylvain that each team had been assigned work that was heavily reliant on the work of one or more other teams; as a result, 75 percent of each team's time was spent resolving dependencies. Sometimes the only person who could do the required work was on another team. Sylvain asked them to figure out the best team and work organization. What evolved was that, during each iteration, the leads would look at the upcoming work and determine the best software developers to be on each team to do a specific subset of the given requirements.

One may ask how that many people can manage themselves. One may as well ask how one manager can manage that many people. What allowed Sylvain to let his developers transition to self-management was the controlled risk. He was never risking more than 30 days of work. As the current approach wasn't working very well, a controlled gamble on his part seemed worthwhile.

Cross-Functionality

As a team self-organizes, people with the best skills will step forward, supported by the other team members. They will discuss how to do something, and each person will go do his or her part. The team members will examine the results frequently to ensure that they all pulled together to create a usable increment.

Cross-functionality is contrary to predictive management, in which the work is laid out in detailed tasks, with each task assigned to a person with a specific skill set. However, this approach doesn't let people collaborate. We have found that software developers create the best solutions when all their knowledge is focused at once on the problem. Their overlapping knowledge is greater than any unique skills one person might have.

Summary

We have described a pilot program that illustrates how you can determine whether empirical software development can help you. The pilot approach not only helps you gain certainty before proceeding but also helps you uncover the issues you will have to deal with.

4

What Can I Do?

IF YOU'VE MADE it this far, you've decided to go further with empirical software development. You may be enamored, you may be intellectually intrigued, or you may crave the benefits demonstrated by the pilot. Regardless, you know it is better than what you have now.

Although many other parts of your organization, such as the sales and financial organizations, operate empirically, this is new to your software developers. Everyone in software development and those who employ them to build products are used to predictive software development. They have probably known it for at least several years, maybe longer. To them, it is the way things are done.

Managers ask what they can do to help make empirical software development succeed. Most people are unfamiliar with applying empiricism to software development. In the following sections, we discuss empirical practices and outlooks that management can help them become aware of.

Practice the Art of the Possible

Empiricism is doing the best you can with what you have. In the past, software development started by creating a plan. Developers were then expected and managed to follow the plan exactly, regardless of the realities they encountered.

49

Empirical software development plans are created just in time. A goal is established, and then the team moves toward that goal, iteration by iteration. The plan is modified as needed based on experience. The path to the goal may be different from what is anticipated, but it is tailored and optimized to the realities that are encountered. The project is complete when the return on investment is optimized. That may be earlier than you expected. For instance, a project may be ended after two iterations when you discover that the goal is unattainable at a reasonable cost. That is a success—a successful avoidance of more wasted money.

Let's look at this further. If F-Secure, a Finnish security software firm, had continued through the whole development effort, the money spent on the last iterations would have been a waste since the product was too late. The team does what is possible. It estimates how many requirements it believes it can turn into an increment. This is an estimate, a forecast; it is not a guarantee or certainty. During the iteration, a team member might become ill, some of the technology might not work, and the software might be trickier than expected. This is complexity in action. At the end of the iteration, you empirically inspect how much functionality was developed. It might be more or less than forecasted. However, you know what was developed and can make decisions about what to do next based on the results. Empiricism does not create certainty; it makes one aware of the possibilities.

F-Secure develops virus detection and security software in Finland for a worldwide market. A partner of F-Secure had requested that they enter a specific segment of the antivirus market to no avail. Finally, he offered to fund the product development. F-Secure developers would develop additional functionality for his company, which would then remarket it under their brand.

F-Secure had used empirical software development for several years. They knew, on average, about how much software their development teams could build in each iteration. Based on this knowledge, they negotiated a plan with the partner. They would create a partial release for an upcoming conference, and shortly after, they would create the first release for the market. Unfortunately, the F-Secure teams assigned to this work created less functionality in the first three iterations than planned. Twenty-five percent of the way to the conference, it was transparent that the product would not be ready in time. It wouldn't be anywhere near ready.

The partner and F-Secure management had been observing the slower-than-hoped-for progress. They stopped all work. Money had been spent, and nothing of value had been created—the goals had not been achieved. However, the partner knew he couldn't have the product in time. He stopped all preparations for the conference, unwound all marketing and sales activities, and saved himself a marketplace embarrassment. The value derived in this project was limiting the loss and not squandering the opportunity.

Many people have a hard time with empiricism. Maybe the team didn't develop what they wanted. Maybe the team didn't develop as much functionality as they wished. A venture capitalist we know had the hardest time. He knew what he wanted to have done each iteration. He would let the team forecast, but he would let them know what he expected. If the team did not do what he expected, he would tell them, "I'm really, really disappointed in you." Somehow, he believed that his wishes would become a reality, that he could make what he wanted come true. All he accomplished was destroying the morale and effectiveness of the team.

Empiricism is the art of the possible, doing the best you can with what you have. This opens up all sorts of possibilities. However, if you think you can decide what you want and push to get it, regardless, you have precluded other possibilities. You are no longer dealing with reality; you are trying to get reality to be what you want, to do your bidding. That might be possible in a simple situation, but it is only demoralizing and frustrating when the problem is complex.

A manager's most important work is helping the people doing the work. Give them a goal and let them work. Remove any impediments that get in their way. Do anything that may make them more effective or productive. Then the organization can capitalize on the fruits of their work.

Demand Transparency and Create an Environment for It to Flourish

You have to have a firm grasp of the real facts to make a solid decision. The data or information you base your decision on must be transparent and clearly understood. In empirical software development, the increment is the clear and transparent information that decisions are based on.

People must feel safe to have crucial conversations, to openly express what they think and feel, and to collaborate with others without reprisal or harm. These conversations are the heart of empiricism. Many workplaces are unsafe. Political agendas and hidden purposes pervert transparency. A manager's biggest job is to create a safe workplace, where people respect one another and feel safe to do their best, whatever that is.

Transparency is value-neutral, meaning it is neither good or bad. Things and increments just are. They may not be what you want, but that means hard decisions are required. To the extent that conversations, requirements, and increments of functionality are deemed good or bad by someone with authority, people will work to show only what is deemed good. They will pervert reality to please the person. At that moment, empirical software development falls apart.

Kronos is a Boston-based developer of enterprise resource time and attendance software. Kronos attempted to employ empirical software development, referred to as agile software development. In 2008, management in the development organization was dissatisfied with progress on the next release. They let the developers know their dissatisfaction and asked them to work harder. The developers wanted to please their managers, so they developed functionality more quickly—except what they developed was of a lower than acceptable quality.

At the end of each iteration, management congratulated the developers on their hard work. However, the increment was not transparent. Management thought the increment was done and usable; it was only partially done and was completely unusable. When Kronos approached the release date, the undone work was discovered. The release date slipped by six months while the developers completed the work.

Count on Your People to Do More

The people on the teams who are doing the work are the people best equipped to figure out how to do it. That thought runs counter to most management teachings. A manager is supposed to set a goal, figure out how to accomplish it, and then get people to follow that plan. However, then everyone is constrained to the experience, insights, and intelligence of the manager as they work.

If the people doing the work are free to devise what to do, they can adapt to the circumstances, to the realities they face. They can share ideas and expertise to come up with the best solutions. They then try an approach, and if it doesn't work, they can try something else. This is self-organization. It applies the collective intelligence of all of the people on the team. They are not constrained to the manager's thinking and are free to do their best work.

The role of the manager with this approach is to set goals, facilitate, and remove obstacles. The manager empowers the people on the team.

Help People Relax Their Desire for Certainty

The world is uncertain. Software development is uncertain. Decisions still need to be made, and the organization that makes the best decisions thrives. Software in 30 days provides solid, actionable information about what is happening at least every 30 days. Each iteration is a constrained gamble. Almost without fail, the team is able to develop some software of value. Even in the worst case, where the team doesn't deliver anything, they have delivered valuable information about what is and isn't possible.

Primavera, based in Philadelphia and now owned by Oracle, develops project management software. The software is used to manage predictive process projects. The founders were aware of the irony that they had to use empirical software processes to build their predictive tools. However, to solve their problems, they had to resort to it.

At the end of the very first iteration, the team and senior management gathered to see a demonstration of the increment. The functionality worked fine. However, the chief technology officer (CTO) pointed out that the team said that it would build seven pieces of functionality. It had built only five. The CTO was uncomfortable. He asked the team to start accumulating statistics of how long it took to do its work. He thought that if these statistics were normalized and aggregated in a database, the team would be more accurate. They could assess the upcoming functionality size with database statistics at the start of the iteration. They would have then known that they could do only five pieces of functionality.

Software development is unpredictable. The past does not predict the future, since software development is different each time. The database would not be useful.

We all want certainty, but it is often unobtainable. However, we can act intelligently, make good decisions, and constrain our risk. That is empirical software development in a nutshell and why short iterations reduce risk.

Summary

The degree of success you have with empirical software development largely depends on the leadership in your organization and how they lead everyone in the above changes.

SECTION

II

How to Produce Software in 30 Days

ORGANIZATIONS WANT TO become more flexible, more creative, more productive, and more profitable. They want to please their customers and outdo their competitors. Many organizations have decided to use Scrum as one of their key strategies. Sometimes it is used for critical work only; sometimes a new development or information technology (IT) organization is created in parallel with the existing waterfall organization. Sometimes the entire enterprise is transformed to become more agile, more flexible, and more competitive. Regardless of what is desired, a change from the normal way of doing things is required. As with most significant change, an unorganized approach, regardless of its intrinsic merits, is doomed to failure. The change to the Scrum approach described in this section of the book is incremental.

We start by introducing you quickly to Scrum. We then have categorized this approach into three steps, each covered in a separate chapter:

1. *Scrum at the project level:* This approach is taken "when necessary" (from the Latin *pro re nata*, or PRN, which means "take when needed"). It is used, for example, when someone requires software within 30 days or less.

Chapter 6 explains how to implement Scrum at the project level with minimum overhead and the quickest results.

2. *Scrum at the capability level:* A software studio, in which Scrum projects are undertaken, is created separate from the rest of the organization. The studio is tasked with creating competitive advantage using Scrum. It operates with a high degree of autonomy and is unhampered by bureaucracy. As the benefits from Scrum become apparent, the studio's use will increase. Chapter 7 describes this step.

3. *Scrum at the enterprise level:* In the enterprise step, the learning from the software studio is extended into the entire organization, to its overall productivity and agility. Chapter 8 explains this step, also covering how to use Scrum to implement Scrum and how to distinguish between talking the Scrum talk and walking the Scrum walk.

5

Getting Started with Scrum

SCRUM IS A framework for managing complex work, such as software development. It is very simple, consisting only of three roles, three artifacts, and five events (Figure 5.1). Scrum binds them together with rules of play.

The team of people that will be developing the software is called the Scrum Team. It consists of the person who wants the software developed (the Product Owner), a manager (the Scrum Master), and the developers. To avoid confusion, there can be only one Product Owner. The Product Owner decides what should be developed in every iteration, or *Sprint* in Scrum terminology, and evaluates the incremental results at the end of every Sprint. The Scrum Master manages the project the Scrum way. Some Scrum Masters are certified in Scrum; some have significant, verifiable experience in using Scrum successfully. Knowing how to manage Scrum Teams and projects is what counts.

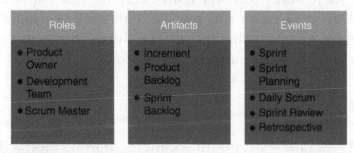

Roles	Artifacts	Events
• Product Owner	• Increment	• Sprint
• Development Team	• Product Backlog	• Sprint Planning
• Scrum Master	• Sprint Backlog	• Daily Scrum
		• Sprint Review
		• Retrospective

Figure 5.1 Scrum Basics

Form the Scrum Team and Plan the Sprint

The first task for the Scrum Master is to find developers to form the Development Team. The people on this team need to have the skills to turn the needs and requirements of the Product Owner (Product Backlog) into working increments of software with every Sprint.

All members of the Scrum Team get together for introductions, discuss the upcoming work, and lay out the logistics for working together. The Scrum Team needs to know the vision (the needed and the hoped-for outcome), what outcomes would signify success and failure, and what the constraints are. The team looks only at the most important requirements and selects the maximum number that have a high likelihood of being developed in the upcoming Sprint. (The developers are skilled at decomposing big requirements into small actionable things that they can develop in a Sprint.)

The developers on the Scrum Team estimate the effort to develop the requirements into completed software functionality. Because they will be doing the work, they should make the estimates. The accuracy of these estimates depends on how long the developers in the team have worked together, how well they understand the technologies involved, and how well they understand the business or problem domain.

When the planning is complete, the developers forecast what work they believe they can do by the end of the Sprint. This is empiricism in action: Set a forecast, see what can actually be developed, and make decisions based on the outcome.

Because of the need to get moving, this short start-up is one day in length. The Scrum Team works together until everyone has a firm grasp of the problem and the approach to it, that is, until everyone knows what will be developed in the upcoming Sprint. The things that aren't explicit will become clear once the team starts creating software.

Sprint to Value

The Scrum Team now starts creating software, starting on the day immediately after the day of Sprint planning. The developers create an increment of software functionality during the first Sprint. It may be larger or smaller than they have forecast. The entire Scrum Team collaborates during the sprint, clarifying the work. The work may have to be redefined, with requirements added or removed as needed, if the Development Team finds that it has time left or the remaining time is inadequate.

Every day during the Sprint, the developers have a 15-minute meeting, called the Daily Scrum, to replan their upcoming work, always striving to deliver what was forecast. To maximize developer productivity, the Sprint objective must be agreed on by both the developers and the Product Owner. They agree that they will build as much of the required software as they can and that they may be redirected with every new Sprint. The Product Owner agrees that the requirements the developers are working on will not change during a Sprint. Anything that wasn't planned (including, for example, bringing developers to customer meetings) waits for the next sprint. Developer productivity arises from not being interrupted. Employing shorter sprints usually accommodates more frequent changes, as is discussed in a later chapter.

Conduct the Sprint Review

At the end of the Sprint, you and the Scrum Master meet with the developers for a Sprint Review. This meeting is never more than four hours in length. The Scrum Team and key stakeholders get together and look at what happened during the prior Sprint and the increment of functionality that emerged during it. The review includes what was done, how much was done, how effectively it was done, and the usefulness of the work. The increment must be completed, meaning the increments must be a complete piece of usable software. Product Backlog items not completely done go back into the Product Backlog as "still to be done." New requirements often arise during the Sprint Review. New opportunities and challenges also arise. Often, just seeing the increment of functionality evokes new ideas

The results of the review can include one or more of the following:

- Start using the increment of functionality.
- Decide what to do during the next Sprint and prepare for it.
- Decide not to proceed. Stop the work.

In this way, risk is limited to one Sprint of investment. Value is delivered at the end of every Sprint, and the next Sprint is formulated. If you are going to proceed with another Sprint, building more increments of software, a Sprint Retrospective is held.

Conduct the Sprint Retrospective

Every member of the Scrum Team strives to improve Sprint by Sprint. The Sprint Retrospective is where the improvements are formulated. This meeting should never exceed four hours.

As a natural break between Sprints, the Sprint Retrospective is when the Scrum Team sits back, reviews what happened during the prior Sprint, and formulates ways to improve their work and the way the work is conducted. The discussion might include:

- Whether or not the team members worked well together and why.
- Whether the team did more or less than it forecast and why.
- Whether the team has all the skills and facilities it needs to do the job.
- Whether or not the developers understood the requirements and why.
- Whether the team was able to complete the Sprint in line with the requirements, and if not, why not?
- What could be improved or dropped in the next increment of functionality.
- What the team thinks of using Scrum.

Next, the team identifies several things to do differently in the upcoming Sprint that will increase creativity, effectiveness, and productivity. In general, Scrum Teams continually improve. This is the Scrum Team's chance to make its work and life better.

Continue Sprinting

The Scrum Team continues through the steps described earlier until the goals are achieved, opportunities are maximized, return on investment is achieved, or an insurmountable obstacle is encountered (Figure 5.2).

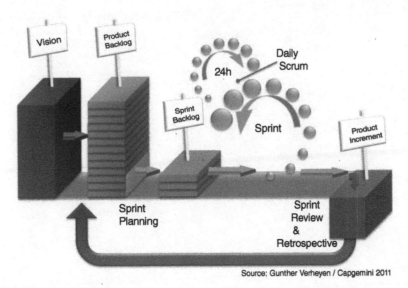

Figure 5.2 Scrum in Action

Summary

Scrum is simple. We've looked at it. We know its parts. We know how to go from planning through delivering. Now we'll look at making Scrum work in your organization.

6

Scrum at the Project Level

USE SCRUM WHEN necessary, such as when you have an immediate opportunity or a catastrophic project. This chapter will help you understand how to start immediately, without fuss or overhead. You will learn how to get value every 30 days.

Organizational impacts need not be considered. Short-term benefits are paramount, not the long-term improvement of the organization. Benefits will accrue rapidly. The Scrum project is conducted in isolation from traditional practices and processes, using only what brings value to the work.

Bottom-Up and Stealth Scrum

Over the past 20 years, many Scrum projects have been run at the bottom of the organization, out of sight. A project team would try Scrum and generate impressive results. Another team would try it, and soon pockets within the organization would be developing software more quickly and more frequently. Pretty soon Scrum projects would appear throughout the organization.

We call this Scrum PRN.[1] Just as the administration of p.r.n. medication is left to the nurse/caregiver or patient's prerogative, Scrum PRN is the answer

---

[1] One translation of *PRN*, or *pro re nata*, is "as circumstances require." The notation *prn* on a prescription means "take when necessary" or "take as needed."

when an important opportunity or critical challenge arises and software is needed quickly. It can be deployed immediately. Exceptions to the usual way of getting things done are allowed in order to meet a crisis or seize an opportunity. Use of Scrum PRN does not require permission. Its authority is the immediate need for software.

Benefits and Discoveries

The cost for a 30-day Sprint can range between $50,000 and $150,000, depending on the size of the Scrum Team, the members' salaries and fringe benefits, and other factors. The return includes:

- *Knowledge about the developers' skill levels:* Through this process, knowledge will be gained about whether the developers can create the needed software functionality and how much can they build during a Sprint.
- *Functionality:* Some functionality can be used at the end of every Sprint, no matter how small the amount. This functionality adds to any previously delivered increments.
- *Replanning:* Investments can be reassessed and replanned for every Sprint. This is called just-in-time planning. As change is anticipated, replanning occurs to accommodate it. Time spent planning things that may never be built is eliminated.

Scrum projects expose everything, both that which we had hoped for and things contrary to our expectations. Scrum dishes it up so that we know what is happening and can make intelligent decisions about what to do next. The benefit is an opportunity to control what happens next, to manage it in workable chunks of investment.

Managing the Work: Burndown Charts

One of Scrum's best features is the information it provides. Management can use this information to maximize value and control risk.

At the end of each Sprint, the work of the developers is tracked, including how many requirements were met and are ready to use. From this, progress relative to the goal can be measured and used, very cautiously, to forecast the future.

The work can be managed using just three variables. First are requirements, the functionality that will deliver the vision. Some are small, some medium, and some large in terms of effort required. Second is time, which is measured in Sprints. Third is work completed, which is measured in usable pieces of functionality delivered.

When requirements transformed into increments of functionality are measured across time, trends emerge. For example, at the beginning of the first Sprint the Development Team has estimated the size of the requirements as 140 units of work. The Development Team delivers 20 units of work in Sprint 1, 40 units of work in Sprint 2, and 40 units of work in Sprint 3. These can be tracked by means of burndown charts. A burndown chart measures the requirements in units of work remaining to be done. This remaining work is calculated at the end of each Sprint. It is equal to the units of work remaining forecast at the beginning of the Sprint LESS the units of work completed and turned into the increment at the end of the Sprint. The work burndown chart for the example project would look like that shown in Figure 6.1

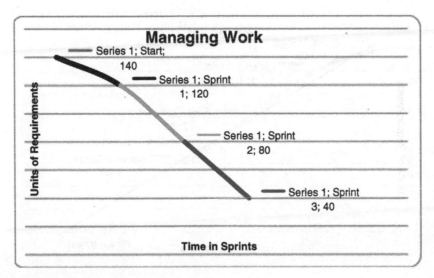

Figure 6.1   Sample Burndown Chart

This provides a picture of the progress made toward having all work completed.

To forecast the future, one can utilize past averages. In the first three Sprints, the average units of requirements completed were 33.3, with a standard deviation of 11.5. A trend line forecasts as shown in Figure 6.2.

This burndown forecasts that the project will be completed by the end of the fourth Sprint (the next Sprint). Of course, developing software is rarely this simple. It is complex work, and more things are unknown than are known. Forecasting software development is a risky business, influenced on any given day by the abilities of the people doing the development, the stability of the technology used, and the marketplace—in which new requirements may emerge suddenly. A trend line loses its validity the further it is projected into the future.

New requirements emerge as the project moves forward. Customers find new needs. When increments are inspected, new possibilities arise. For instance, with 140 units of requirements at the start of the first Sprint, if 20, 40, and then 40 more units of requirements emerge and are added to the Product Backlog in each of the first three Sprints, the burndown will be flat, falsely giving the impression that no work was completed (Figure 6.3). This occurs because exactly as much work is found and added to the backlog every Sprint as the Development Team completes.

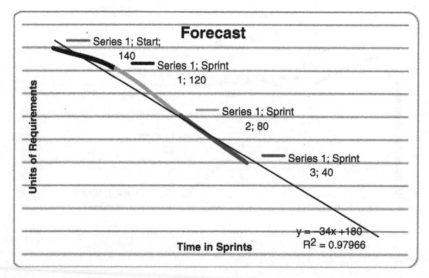

Figure 6.2   Sample Forecast

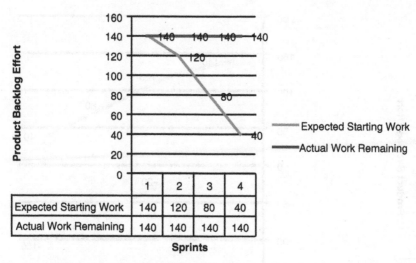

Figure 6.3 Actual vs. Anticipated Burndown

To retain the utility of the burndown slope, a new "net" baseline is calculated: [(starting baseline + additional requirements of work) − (completed requirements of work) = new net baseline]. This new net baseline is shown in Figure 6.4. It helps us project that the project will likely be complete much later than the previously anticipated fourth Sprint.

With Scrum, we can stop funding further Sprints as soon as the remaining requirements are deemed to be of low value. At this point, the software is released and feedback is elicited from the users. The additional functionality the users request is often not something that was originally envisioned by the Scrum Team. With this feedback in hand, the next release is reformulated to include the user-requested requirements and to exclude those that were still on the to-do list but not included in the first release and not desired by the users.

The Standish Group estimates that 50 percent of all features of software are scarcely or never used.[2] As an example, 80 percent of customers use only 14 percent of the functionality in the massive hp.com site.[3] So to optimize value, the Project Owner must decide when to stop Sprinting—to stop further

---

[2] J. Johnson, *Chaos Manifesto: The Laws of CHAOS and the CHAOS 100 Best PM Practices* (Boston: The Standish Group, 2011), 25.

[3] Related to Ken Schwaber on November 10, 2009, at a Scrum presentation at Hewlett-Packard in Palo Alto, California, by John Sawyer.

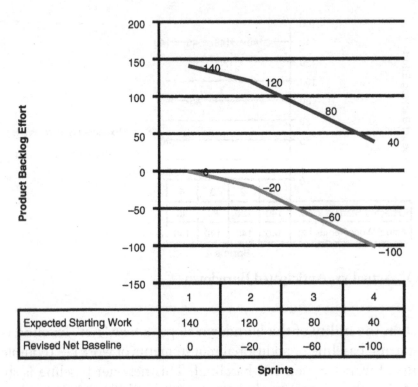

Figure 6.4 Net Baseline Reflects Changed Product Backlog

development and not deliver a product with low-value functionality. With just this tactic, projects can take only 40 percent of the time they would otherwise consume. This productivity is yours to have just by paying attention to the value of what you are having developed.

Don't Ignore On Complexity—Always Keep Your Eyes Open

We know that we can use Scrum to meet a challenge or take advantage of an opportunity. Before starting the first Sprint we often want to know how long the project will take and what it will cost. We can derive starting estimates by extrapolating the results of the first several Sprints. For example, say we develop 20 units of functionality in two Sprints. We estimate that the system as we envision it has 220 units of functionality. We have another 180 units to build. At 20 units per Sprint, we will be finished in nine more iterations. If we add or subtract functionality while we develop the software, we will divide the remaining work by our per-Sprint functionality delivery rate.

Of course, one should use extreme care when extrapolating from the past to create a forecast. Extrapolation is the process of constructing new data points. It is similar to the process of interpolation, which constructs new points between known points, but the results of extrapolations are less meaningful and are subject to greater uncertainty. We know that software development is complex, with more unknown than is known. We can extrapolate, but we must verify. At the end of every iteration, we verify where we really are, not where we extrapolated we would be. Reality is firmer ground than expectations.

The problem with new opportunities is that they are new. The ways to exploit them generally are either to create something new or to use a new twist on an old approach. Either way, there is a lot of new stuff to think through, solutions to fashion, and software to write or repurpose. Traditionally, we are asked to do the thinking prior to starting the software development. This is called requirements planning, and it results in a product document or marketing requirements document. The problem is that we don't know exactly what we want. Even if we have really solid ideas, the best approach usually emerges as we proceed. Because the definition of complex problems is that there are more things that we do not know than we do know, upfront planning is inherently difficult and full of error and omission. With Scrum, we plan as we go, finding what we need as the project progresses. Predictability comes from timely decision making based on real results. Although we project time and cost at the beginning of the project, we constantly evaluate it as we move forward. Traditional projects forecast time and cost at the beginning of the project also, but do not provide any effective data for replanning until the project is at least 90 percent complete.

Sprint Length

Organizations that use Scrum tend to use 30-day Sprints, but Scrum also permits shorter Sprints as well as monthly Sprints. The longer sprints are used for more stable situations, and the shorter Sprints are used for more opportunistic or challenging situations.

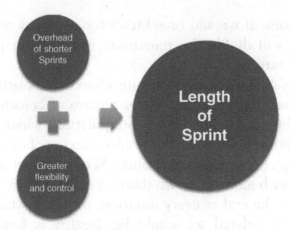

Figure 6.5   Variables Affecting Sprint Length

The best length of the Sprint for your project is made by evaluating the following (Figure 6.5):

- Overhead of shorter sprints
- Greater flexibility and control
- Length of sprint

Sprints are never longer than one month.

Reasons for Shorter Sprints

Four 1-week Sprints provide more flexibility and control than one 30-day Sprint. These are some of the variables that may affect your choice of Sprint length:

1. *Volatile market environment:* The length of the Sprint determines how often you can redirect and replan a product. The market for the product may be either new or volatile. Other organizations and competitors are also introducing products. You want to maintain more flexibility to accommodate rapid response to opportunities. Or, you may not want to invest as much in any feature before having an opportunity to change direction.

2. *Volatile team:* Scrum Teams sometimes require up to one year to become proficient, or they may never become proficient. Shorter Sprints give

everyone a close look at the dynamics of the team so that issues can be rapidly addressed and productivity enhanced.

3. *Volatile technology:* Whenever new technologies are used, more information about their utility and value is needed early. In newer products, the capability of newer technologies is often the determinant for success. Try them out by attempting to build small pieces of functionality. See how they work, if they work, and if they support the manner in which the system has to work. For instance, if the product has to support many simultaneous users or have a high degree of security, find out very early if the technology supports this. If not, you can either reformulate the project or cancel it.

4. *Establishment of velocity stability:* The best way to forecast the cost of a project is to review past productivity on similar projects, identical technologies, and teams that have worked together for a long time. To the extent that similar previous projects are not available, the next best way to project the cost is to run shorter Sprints. As the developers learn to work with one another on your domain with the technologies, they will begin to establish a stable velocity, or amount of functionality they can build every Sprint. When this begins to stabilize to a reasonable standard deviation, you can carefully forecast the capacity of the Development Team against the projected work to determine cost and date of delivery. Remember, however, that a forecast is not a guarantee.

5. *Provision of a a learning experience:* People like to be successful. When people learn to ride a bicycle or to ski or ice skate, they usually try for short periods of time at first. Failure can be evaluated and changes made. Then they attempt again. Shorter Sprints facilitate learning.

6. *Risk control:* The desired return on investment of the project may be unobtainable. When the marketplace is volatile or unknown, the technologies are unproven, and the people are new to the work, gathering the cost and benefit information early is critical, and shorter Sprints provide this information, making it possible to control the project more frequently. Less money is invested before finding out that change or cancellation is called for.

In general, longer Sprints are used when there is less risk, volatility, or uncertainty. For instance, the product or system is going to be used internally. Or

Sprint Length	Time for Sprint Meetings	Total Sprint Meeting Days	Increased Cost
30 days	2 days	2 days	
2 weeks	1.8 days * 2	3.6 days	$10,700
1 week	1.5 days * 4	6 days	$40,000

Figure 6.6   Cost of Shorter Sprints

perhaps the pressure for the system is increased capability or lower costs, not competitive pressure. In either or similar cases, 30-day Sprints may be more than adequate.

Reasons Against Shorter Sprints

Two 2-week Sprints cost more than one 30-day Sprint. Twice as many Sprint Planning, Review, and Retrospective Meetings will occur. The Scrum Team will have to formulate a new design twice as often. The natural ramp-up and wind-down from Sprints will happen twice as often.

The price of shorter Sprints is the increased time needed for planning and review. You can consider this the cost of opportunity or the cost of insurance. Figure 6.6 shows sample figures for the time needed for planning Sprints of different lengths. For instance, the times needed within 30 days for the Sprint meetings are compared for the one 30-day Sprint, the equivalent four 1-week Sprints, and the other equivalents. The Sprint Meetings are the Planning, Review, and Retrospective. Daily Scrum costs are the same. The cost of the Scrum Team used is $200,000 per 30-day Sprint.

Given the greater predictability, control, and flexibility, many organizations find the overhead costs of shorter Sprints acceptable.

Do Not Attempt Sprints of These Lengths

When Sprints are less than one week long, the time to turn requirements into usable functionality is often inadequate. Development Teams find it hard to build anything that is usable or provides management information in less than one week.

We recommend that Sprints are never longer than thirty days or one month. When Sprints are longer than 30 days (or one month), these problems occur:

1. The stakeholders lose attention and forget about the project.
2. As the number of requirements increases, the overall complexity increases in a fashion greater than linear. To manage the increased complexity and remember prior decisions, Development Teams require more documentation and design facilities.
3. The amount of information to review and absorb and then make decisions overwhelms the effectiveness of Scrum's short meetings.

Keep Sprints within a Project the Same Length

When possible, keep the length of all the Sprints for a development project the same, from the first until the last Sprint. Software Development Teams do their best when they can pace their work, because they develop a rhythm. After six 30-day Sprints, developers develop a pattern of how to formulate and do their work. If you switch to a one-week Sprint, they initially approach it using their 30-day pattern, which is too stretched out. They often find that they forecast more work than they can do for the first three Sprints after the change in length. The team has to reset its pace each time the length of the Sprint changes, and the members usually lose productivity when this happens. Consistent Sprint length promotes productivity.

Of course, there may be a compelling reason to change the length of the Sprints within a project. You may find the results of a Sprint to be a disaster. Maybe the Development Team didn't work together well, the requirements weren't understood, too much time was spent on one problem, or other problems occurred. These problems become transparent sooner with shorter Sprints. Redirecting work or reformulating the Development Team may have been done sooner. The loss would have been less. Change Sprint lengths as needed, but do so no more often than needed. If you keep changing Sprint lengths, everyone tends to lose focus, clarity, and an understanding of what is possible. Software development is emergent and complex, so simplify whenever possible.

An Example of PRN Scrum Projects

Fidelity Investments used Scrum in 1997 to provide web-based capabilities to its customers. Charles Schwab and E-Trade customers were already managing their funds online, but Fidelity's customers could not. At the time, Fidelity was a rigidly waterfall organization. Multiple attempts had been made to provide web-based capability; each had failed. In desperation, Fidelity turned to Scrum. Within months, the first instance of Fidelity.com was up and running. Within 18 months, investors were as happy with Fidelity.com as with any competitive offering. Success was declared, and Scrum was decommissioned.

Fidelity learned to use Scrum for its critical needs. The next seven times that Fidelity critically needed software to be developed, it created Scrum projects. However, Fidelity did not benefit as much as it could have if it had built on its experience. Each Scrum project could have been more effective than the previous one. However, Fidelity has chosen to use Scrum only in times of emergency, PRN.

The Next Chapter

In the next chapter, we explain how to progressively increase the benefits of Scrum by means of a sustained, measurable approach that minimizes disruption while maximizing benefits to the organization.

7

Develop a Scrum Capability

A STEP UP from Scrum at the project level, a Scrum software studio, is an established, ongoing facility in which Scrum software projects can be launched rapidly. The software studio is a new, separate organization within your larger organization. Some organizations use a studio to run all their projects. Alternatively, the studio could be a place where only projects of a certain complexity, size, or risk are undertaken. Like PRN Scrum, the studio step avoids the difficulty and potential failure of attempting enterprise-wide change.

The software studio also is known as the software factory.[1] However, *factory* implies that repetitive, standardized, simple work is done. Software development is not repetitive, simple work.

The Studio Is a Learning Organization

Most organizations that adopt Scrum require several years to begin fully reaping the most significant benefits. At the very start, their productivity is better and the projects are more manageable than before. However, the greater benefits of quality, value, and bottom-up intelligence arrive slowly. The organization needs to systematically build on what is learned in each project. The

[1] J. Greenfield, "The Case for Software Factories," Microsoft Corporation, MSDN Library (Redmond, Washington, July 2004).

studio is a place where knowledge for creating a sustainable advantage is rapidly amassed and benefits accrue.[2]

All work in the studio is based on Scrum. Each development project contributes to the knowledge, expertise, productivity, and value of all the projects that follow. As more projects are undertaken in the studio, better facilities, practices, and knowledge accumulate. As a result, each successive project is more productive and has higher value.

The studio has its own culture, incorporating changes and support necessary for software development and management using Scrum. Anyone who wants to use this culture to develop systems or products can do so; however, he or she must learn and conform to its cultural norms. Only people who are willing to adopt Scrum use the studio. The others are left in place to continue doing work in the way they always have.

The Studio Manager

The first step is to find someone to establish and manage the studio. The studio manager is also a Scrum Master. His or her job is to get the studio going, with the best facilities at hand. The studio manager:

- Should have a background that includes several years as a Scrum Master, the manager in a Scrum environment.
- Should understand software development.
- Should be skilled in change management and facilitation.
- Will provide training and coaching for developers in the studio.
- Will ensure that Scrum Masters working on projects in the studio are doing their jobs well.
- Will help optimize project results.
- Will progressively improve the studio facilities so that successive projects become more efficient and effective.

The studio manager scours the software industry for the best, most cost-justifiable software, practices, and automated tools. The software and tools

---

[2] I. Nonaka and H. Takeuchi, *The Knowledge-Creating Company: How Japanese Companies Create the Dynamics of Innovation* (London: Oxford University Press, 1995).

may range from rudimentary to sophisticated, depending on how long the studio has been running and improving.

The studio manager's goal is to provide an environment that supports development of competitive, creative software for the best possible cost. At a minimum, the goal of the studio is to make it easier to launch new Scrum projects.

Training and Terms of Use

Learning something as different as Scrum can be difficult. People must be willing to learn a new way of managing and developing software. This learning is successful only for those who are willing and eager to learn and to invest the sweat equity to do so. If a department plans to run all of its projects in the studio, everyone involved must commit to working in a different way.

First-time users of the studio go through a two-day Scrum Foundations course. They are trained in Scrum and its underlying theory and principles. They are run through numerous boot camp simulations until they understand the feel and flow of a Scrum project. Ground rules, meeting times, Sprint length, and so on, are established.

Ways of working are formalized and described. New techniques may be required for the following:

- Compensation for team rather than individual performance
- Reporting structures and performance reviews
- Conflict resolution
- How to deal with troublesome team members
- Escalation of impediments and needs

An overview of the studio facilities is also presented so that team members know what the facilities are, how to use them, and how to get help.

A team-building session will be conducted. Team members get to know one another by engaging in some problem-solving exercises and are taught how to work through conflicts, which are not uncommon in self-organizing teams in which people where different ideas abound.

1. Every project will adhere to Scrum processes and its principles of empiricism, bottom-up intelligence, and self-organization.
2. Every project will have a Scrum Development Team with a Product Owner, Scrum Master, and no more than nine developers.
3. The Scrum Master must be experienced in managing Scrum projects. To the extent that he or she is not, the person will accept guidance from Studio Scrum coaches.
4. The Product Owner will actively work with the team to formulate requirements, inspect work, inspect increments, and empirically adapt in order to optimize project value and achieve its vision or purpose. This is a hands-on role.
5. The Scrum (development) Team will consist of software developers with all the skills needed to create an increment of potentially usable functionality, based on the Product Owner's requirements.
6. Throughout the project, previous reporting relationships will be held in abeyance.
7. Each increment will conform to the Scrum definitions of "transparent" and "complete."
8. The Scrum Team will use modern engineering practices and tools provided by the Studio and will receive training in how to use them, if necessary.
9. The project will conform to the standards of the organization and to the policies, procedures, and standards of the Studio.
10. To the greatest extent possible, the Scrum Team will be collocated within the Studio. The members will work full time on the project.
11. The Scrum Team will take advantage of the Studio's metrics to assist it in managing its work.
12. The Scrum Team members will participate in adding to the Studio's body of knowledge based on their experiences in working on the project.

I agree to the Terms of Use set forth above.

Signed_____ Date_____

Figure 7.1 Terms of Studio Use

People participating on Scrum Teams in the studio sign a terms of use agreement to use the studio's facilities. The agreement provides them with an understanding of what will be expected of them. Figure 7.1 shows a typical agreement.

As new Scrum Teams request to use the studio, their backgrounds, experiences, and skills are evaluated. Their projects also will be evaluated to determine how critical they are and their potential value and time frames. A support plan will be constructed from this information that balances the resources and support in the studio. External support may be employed but is a last alternative.

Studio Facilities

Initially, a studio tends to be bare bones, with more coaching help than anything else. As the studio manager measures and reports benefits to management, investments may be made in facilities that increase the studio's utility. These facilities can enable any project developed in the studio. Often, they are not present in a mainstream software development environment. They include the following:

1. *Work facilities:* Scrum Teams thrive in open facilities that support team collaboration. This means a space in which Scrum Team members can freely interact while developing software and have enough room at each person's area for two or three people to work together. The chairs should be comfortable and the worktables easily moveable. Internet, network, and development servers should already be in place, preloaded with the development tools that the Scrum Team will employ. Hardware also includes projectors/electronic outputs (large TVs) in meeting areas and plenty of whiteboards. There should be space available for visitors or temporary team members. It may be necessary or advisable to reconfigure the space, based on usage patterns and changing needs.

2. *Software development tools and practices:* The Scrum Team must have a completely automated development environment so that as soon as new software is developed or changed, it can be tested to see how it works. Tests may be large, such as functional tests, or small, such as code unit tests. Critical tests are for stability, performance, and security. Lean-quality techniques are employed, in which quality is built in, rather than tested for once the functionality is completed. The Development Team will define the product in terms of the tests, or the things it has to do and how it has to do them. Then it will program the software to pass those tests. If any test fails, the developers stop until the cause of failure is corrected. Incomplete or defective work costs money to correct; as more work is accumulated on top of it, the cost, or technical debt, mounts. It increases more than linearly. The Development Team not only must run tests to ensure that what

it develops works as required, but must also apply all previous tests to ensure that the entire system is not compromised.

3. *Planning and reporting:* A full set of standardized planning, control, risk management, and reporting policies and procedures are available at the studio. Templates will be provided. Scrum Teams must conform to them.

Change and Conundrum

As with a single Scrum project, the Scrum studio implements the cultural changes required for empiricism and self-organization. This is not always easy; Scrum is different. Scrum is a conundrum for everyone. It is unquestionably better than predictive development, but the habits of the past are hardwired. Only practice and insights into the benefits help people make the change from predictive to empirical processes. To help define the conundrum, we devised the instrument shown in Figure 7.2.

In the first part of the instrument, we ask the respondents to review the assertions that they have learned about Scrum from best practices, and sometimes just from common sense. We ask them to indicate whether they agree with, somewhat agree, don't know, or do not agree with the assertions.

If a manager agrees with most of these assertions, he or she can probably commit to Scrum. This means that the manager will not rely on traditional practices that can distract the team, reduce its creativity and initiative, and reduce its productivity. The manager will not make commitments on behalf of a team about how much it can do by a certain date and then try to convince the team that these commitments are attainable. The manager will not make task assignments, tell the team members how to do their work or how to schedule it, or push the team members to work harder so that they can meet the commitments made by the manager. In short, the conundrum is being aware of one thing and acting in a different way. The conundrum is change by reconciling intellectual understanding with day-to-day actions.

Managing by the Numbers

All projects in the studio are assessed by means of metrics. A standardized, comprehensive set of metrics is used for any projects undertaken in the studio.

Area	Agree, Agree Somewhat, Don't Know, or Do Not Agree	Assertion
Motivation		People are most productive when they manage their own work.
Motivation		People take their commitments more seriously than other people's commitments for them.
Motivation		People have many creative moments when they are not actively working.
Motivation		People always do the best they can.
Motivation		Under pressure to "work harder," people, especially software developers, automatically and increasingly reduce the quality of their work.
Teams		Teams are more productive than the same number of individuals working alone.
Teams		Products are more robust when a team has the cross-functional skills to see the product from many perspectives, including support, maintenance, development, quality, marketability, and usability.
Teams		Changes in team composition lower productivity for a time.
Performance		Teams and people do their best work when they are not interrupted.
Performance		Teams improve most when they solve their own problems, learning as they do so.
Performance		Face-to-face, open communications are the best way for teams to communicate.

Figure 7.2 Opinions Survey

The Scrum Team uses these metrics to track and improve its performance. The Scrum Team also uses the metrics to create project and management reports.

The metrics are amalgamated into an overall studio dashboard that tracks project histories and reflects trends. These metrics also are used to assess the costs and benefits of the studio and for evaluating and justifying requests to fund

Figure 7.3   The Project Dashboard

studio improvements. Enterprise management can use the aggregated metrics to determine the overall return on investment (ROI) of the studio and to determine whether its use should be expanded or contracted. Figure 7.3 shows the primary metrics on the dashboard. Each may have many subordinate metrics.

1. *Productivity* is the number of units of business functionality that are developed for a specified amount of money (e.g., per $100,000 invested). Productivity is also called velocity. This is not a measure of value, just of the amount of functionality produced. Initially, an arbitrary unit of functionality is identified and measured. The size is measured in function points, an objective and abstract measurement for software.[3] Function points are uniform and can be applied elsewhere within the system or product or to any other system. All other functionality is assessed relative to this base unit. This measurement (the measurement of the size of the unit of functionality in function points) becomes the normalized studio metric. The base unit requires calibration periodically to ensure consistency.

2. *Quality* is measured in defects in relation to the studio's standard size of work. A Scrum Team develops increments of software functionality. At some point, the Product Owner wants to implement this functionality. From the day that the unit of functionality is given to the Product Owner

---

[3] A. J. Albrecht, "Measuring Application Development Productivity," Proceedings of the Joint SHARE, GUIDE, and IBM Application Development Symposium, Monterey, California, October 14–17 (Armonk, New York: IBM Corporation, 1979), 83–92.

until three months of customer usage of the functionality have passed, the number of defects is counted.

3. *Value* is the measure of how valuable the delivered functionality is to the organization. It is a measure of the effectiveness (a percentage) of each dollar spent on software development that creates value for the organization. The value metric does not include the marketplace value. The marketplace value reflects the return side of the ROI metric, which is not part of this discussion. On average, less than 10 percent of each dollar spent on software development in an organization is spent on valuable new development. The rest is frittered away. A significant percentage is spent on maintaining and sustaining existing systems. Another significant amount is spent developing functionality that isn't used very often. Still more of the dollar is spent on creating software that might be useful elsewhere but not within the organization that is paying for it.

A studio dashboard reflects a trend in increasing productivity and quality, as shown in Figure 7.4.

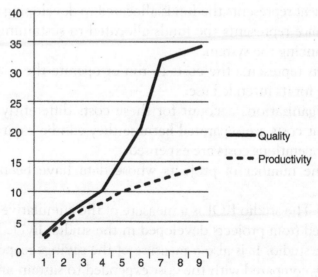

Figure 7.4 Productivity, Quality Dashboard

A studio dashboard next reflects a trend in increasing value and ROI, as shown in Figure 7.5.

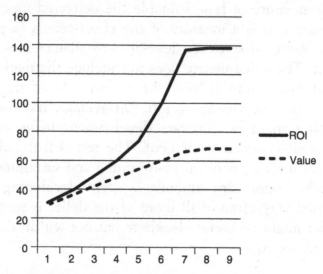

Figure 7.5 Value and Return on Investment Dashboard

Several other metrics may be considered, as follows:

1. *Cost of ownership:* A software system or product has three costs to the development organization, which represent the system's total cost of ownership:
   - *Development* represents the funds allocated to developing the system.
   - *Maintenance* represents the funds allocated to sustaining, maintaining, and enhancing the system.
   - *Operations* represents the costs to run or operate the system while it is available for its intended use.

   Most organizations account for these costs differently. For instance, development costs are separated because they can be capitalized. Maintenance and operations costs are expensed.

2. *Projects:* The number of projects whose data have been aggregated is displayed.

3. *Studio ROI:* The studio ROI is a measure of the cumulative return or total value derived from projects developed in the studio divided by the cost of running the studio. It is also a measure of the savings reaped by improved productivity compared with the cost expended to sustain and enhance the studio. Many organizations do not know the productivity of their software

development organizations, especially in terms of business functionality delivered. The Scrum studio often is forced to create the first measurements of productivity. These are used as baselines for all subsequent improvement.

Figure 7.6 shows some examples of measurements that could be made in a studio.

Decisions made during the development of a product have profound impacts on the cost of ownership of a system. Consider the following impacts:

- Functionality that will receive low usage still must be maintained for the life of the software system and will increase the operational costs.
- The quality of software produced during development dictates the cost to maintain the system and the cost of further enhancements. Lower-quality software is more difficult to enhance than higher-quality software and leaves a legacy of increasing costs to an organization.
- Maintainability and sustainability of the software can be a constraint on the life and utility of the software. Many organizations have been unable to compete, even using Scrum, when the underlying software is in bad shape and the developers who built it are gone.

You are probably used to many metrics being available, such as "earned value." These metrics were very important to you because you had no other way to

Quarter	Productivity	Quality	Value	Studio Return	# of Projects
1	2	0.7	30	1	1
2	5	0.7	35	4	4
3	7	1.0	42	8	8
4	8	2.0	48	12	12
5	10	5.0	54	20	20
6	11	10.0	60	40	40
7	12	20.0	66	70	120
8	13	20.0	68	70	260
9	14	20.0	68	70	560

Figure 7.6 Studio Dashboard Trends

assess the progress and ongoing risk of a software development project. Scrum replaces those metrics with solid, tangible evidence at the end of every Sprint. You have a solid increment of functionality that can immediately be used. All measurements are subordinate to the value and cost of that functionality.

Metrics Depend on Transparency

You've come to Scrum because you want to know what is going on. You want to manage the work for your organization's benefit and your customers' value. The material that Scrum provides to you is:

1. You know how much software functionality remains to be built. Even after you make many changes, you can always project what remains to be done.
2. You know what functionality has been done. Functionality done is like money well spent. It is bankable.
3. You know how much functionality has been done in the last several Sprints. This provides you with a forecast of how long it will take to build the remaining functionality. You remember that this is complex work and the future may change, but some idea is better than no idea.
4. You can take one or more increments of functionality that are done and start using them, realizing value early.

Everything else that Scrum provides to you is gravy compared with this information. You can build productivity, quality, great places to work, engaged customers, and market share. But first, you have to know what you are doing. The transparency of the increment and what it consists of are the foundations.

A Done, Complete Increment of Functionality

At the end of a Sprint, you have an increment of one or more requirements, done and ready to use. Beat it up and make sure it doesn't fall apart. Make sure its quality is good enough for real-world use. Try the increment with it in combination with all previous increments. A done, completed increment is something you can use.

If the increment ever doesn't work and cannot be immediately deployed and used, don't accept it. Tell the developers to reestimate in order to include all the work needed to actually finish it. Then put it back in the Product Backlog.

Opacity Instead of Transparency

We had an experience with the consequences of lack of transparency early in 2002 at a major energy company. Scrum was piloted in one department, whose manager, David, was enthusiastic about the transparency Scrum would provide. Unfortunately, David didn't make sure the increments were done and usable. He didn't even know that he should do so. This is his story.

David needed to automate his department's receipt of property title changes. His department processed and paid royalties to the people who owned the land of interest at the start of each fiscal year. David had to make sure the information was current. He was responsible for the property in the United States and Canada.

All of the title information that his department currently received was in the form of printouts or property change papers. The volume was becoming overwhelming, and David wanted to automate the feeds and royalty payment process.

David decided to have his developers use Scrum to build the system. Not only would the completed product allow him to stay on top of progress, but he could use parts of the functionality as they became available if it made sense.

By the end of the third Sprint, the developers had automated the receipt and integration of title changes from one province in Canada. They demonstrated it using SQL, a technical database query language. David was delighted. He said that he wanted the developers to teach his staff SQL. Most of their backlog was from that province, and the automation would rapidly bring them up to date.

The Development Team told David that he couldn't use the increments of functionality yet. David was incredulous. The team was supposed to be building increments of software that he could use whenever he chose. He had seen the first increment, the second increment, and the third increment. He wanted to start using them to ease the business backlog. He wanted to get some early benefits while development continued.

The Development Team told David that the increments were done for demonstration, but not for use. There were a number of outstanding issues that precluded its use in normal business operations. For instance, the data was not stable and the database would sometimes lose information and become corrupt.

David asked how much more work the developers had to do before he could use the first three increments. The developers estimated another two Sprints were needed to make the increments usable. He told them to go ahead and get it ready for his department's use.

David then had another, harder conversation with the Development Team. He expressed disappointment that progress was not transparent. He felt embarrassed that he had touted Scrum, yet what he had seen was not real. He also let them know that he was doubly embarrassed because he had been reporting progress as though he did know what was happening.

What People Thought Was Happening

Before starting the project, David and the Scrum Team had developed a plan for the system. David made sure everyone knew the plan and that it represented the best possible forecast. He told everyone that he would show them real progress against the plan at the end of every monthly Sprint. Figure 7.7 shows the planned burndown and the reported progress for at the end of the first three Sprints. They were identical.

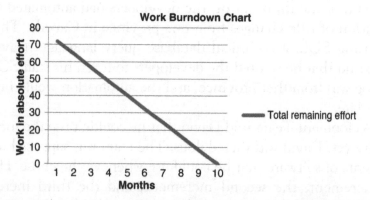

Figure 7.7 The Plan and Reported Progress to the End of the Third Sprint Are the Same

What Had Happened

The developers on the Scrum team had only just begun using Scrum. They understood iterations, increments, Sprints, Daily Scrums, and the rest of the words. However, they didn't understand the importance of transparency and completed increments. They had used the waterfall process previously. With that approach, the software wasn't pulled together until the end of the project. The developers figured they would do the same with Scrum. They would build as much as they could each Sprint. When David wanted to use the software, they would have a period of time when they would make it work. He could then use it.

The Development Team had planned the project with David based on its current skills. They weren't skilled enough to build complete increments every Sprint. They were just learning new engineering practices and required development tools were ordered but not yet being used. They were not yet professionally capable of building a completed increment within one Sprint or building increments that added to previous build increments, as shown in Figure 7.8. At the project outset, they figured they would make the increments truly usable when all Sprints were completed.

David understood transparency and predictability. The Development Team understood only the general concepts of Scrum. They applied the irregularity of waterfall development within Scrum.

Transparency of the increment should have allowed David to manage risk and gain predictability. At the start of the project, David established a release

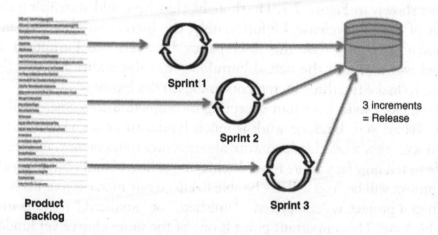

Figure 7.8 Incremental progress toward usable functionality

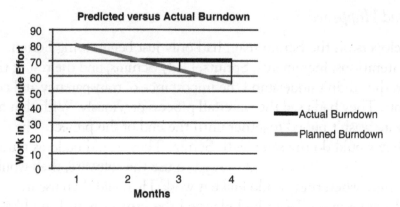

Figure 7.9   Actual versus Planned Completed Work

plan with the Scrum Team. After Sprint 1, he would assess progress toward the goal by inspecting what he thought was a usable increment. He made a decision about what to do in Sprint 2 based on the incremental progress toward the goal. If he had thought the progress was inadequate, he could have cancelled the project. However, since the increment was not transparent, he couldn't effectively make this decision.

When the Development Team estimated the work that was "undone" for the first three Sprints, it added another 14 units of work. The discrepancy between the plan and actual at the end of the third month reflects those "hidden" 14 units of work, as shown in Figure 7.9.

At the end of Sprint 3, David believed that 30 percent of the total was done, as shown in Figure 7.7. He thought that he could start using that 30 percent of the total release. Unfortunately, the increment weren't complete. As shown in Figure 7.9, the discrepancy between the burndown David believed was true and the actual burndown was the additional two Sprints required to make the three increments usable to the business.

If you, like David, ever start accepting incomplete increments, it will come back to haunt you. Undone work is much harder to finish when it has been covered with new work. Undone work also obscures transparency, making it impossible to tell how far you are toward achieving your goal and what the real costs of the project will be. You will not be able to effectively manage your investment.

When a project is "completed," "finished," or "finalized," there is nothing left to be done. This important point is one of the more elusive yet fundamental requirements of Scrum.

An Analogy

In cold climates, when the temperature drops, the pipes in houses often start knocking. Whenever you turn the water on at the tap or use the washer or dishwasher, whenever the heating system starts up, the pipes start banging against one another, against the framing, and against the walls. Sometimes they sound like a jackhammer, especially when they start knocking in the middle of the night. Knocking pipes are hard to fix. They rattle because they weren't properly secured. When they become loose and knock, precisely locating them is difficult. The knocking may be happening at a different place from the insecure pipe. Over time, they become looser. It is difficult to find the exact place where they should have been secured, as the noise may be located a short distance away. Frequently, you have to make a large hole in the wall, remove any insulation, and start looking. Then, with a little luck, you can secure the pipe properly. The cost of securing a pipe correctly when it is installed differs minimally from securing it incorrectly. The cost of securing it once the building already has been constructed is much higher.

Each increment of software should be as solid as a properly installed pipe. If we build more increments of software functionality on top of it, we do not want to have to dig back in to fix something that doesn't work properly. Fixing something after it has been built proves to be very expensive. This is known as technical debt.

Eliminating Technical Debt to Get Ready-to-Use Increments

Many of the Scrum Development Teams with which we have worked were initially unable to develop ready-to-use increments of software by the end of a Sprint. Transparency wasn't required from them in the past, so they often do not have the technical skill or adequate tools to rapidly build transparent software functionality.

Table 7.1 presents in the first column the typical work a development team does to turn Product Backlog requirements into working functionality. The second column, labeled "usual," represents units of work that Development Teams are used to doing prior to the end of a predictive, traditional project for each item of work in the first column. For instance, the developers are used to spending twelve units of work doing requirements analysis. They are used to

Table 7.1　Definition of Done

Work to Be Done	Usual	Done
Requirements analysis	12	25
Design of architectural components	10	15
Design review	2	5
Design of tests (system, user acceptance, integration)	4	10
Design review	0	3
Design of documentation	1	2
Design review	0	1
Refactoring of existing design	4	8
Design of unit tests for new code	1	3
Design of unit tests for code to be refactored	0	3
Writing of new code	7	10
Writing of refactored code	2	6
Code review (or pair programming)	0	4
Writing of functional tests	4	8
Writing of integration tests	2	4
Writing of documentation	2	4
Unit test code	0	2
Identifying and rectifying defects	0	2
Subsystem/team build	2	6
Identifying and rectifying defects	1	1
Unit test for subsystem/team code	0	2
Identifying and rectifying defects	2	5
System/integration build	1	1
Identifying and rectifying defects	0	2
System, functional tests	1	2
Identifying and rectifying defects	1	4
Integration tests	1	2

Work to Be Done	Usual	Done
Identifying and rectifying defects	2	5
Performance tests	1	3
Identifying and rectifying defects	1	2
Security tests	1	2
Identifying and rectifying defects	0	2
Regression test	3	6
Identifying and rectifying defects	4	8
Documentation test	0	2
Identifying and rectifying defects	0	1
Total Work per Product Backlog Item	71	171
Technical Debt per PBI	100	0

doing ten units of work designing architectural components. These are relative numbers, indicating that developers take two more units of work to do the former, or 20 percent more work than the latter.

The third column, labeled "done," represents units of work that are required to create complete, transparent increments of functionality for each item of work in the first column. The total for transparent increments is 171 units of work. Most developers are used to completing only 71 of those units of work when they transition to empirical Scrum projects, as shown in the "usual" column. They are used to leaving behind 100 units of work for every piece of functionality they build. Sprint by Sprint, this undone work accumulates exponentially until the end of the project.

Before you start your first Sprint, have the Scrum Master and Development Team assess Table 7.1. Have them create a new table appropriate for the type of software that you want them to build. Then, have them figure out how to complete all of the work before they start the first Sprint. To see if they have done so, ask to start using one or more increments of functionality at the end of any Sprint. If they say that you can't, or you try and it doesn't do the job, the developers on the team need more training and practice.

Adobe and Technical Debt

Adobe Premiere Pro is the industry-leading suite of graphic design, video editing, and web development applications targeted to the video production marketplace. BBC programs and *The Tonight Show* are produced using it. Division Vice President Steve Warner manages Premiere Pro. Peter Green was the program manager of its Creative Suite. Emerging standards and demand for new capabilities had them under the gun to put out significant new releases quickly.

Premier Pro CS3 (Creative Suite, release 3.0) was released in July 2007. Traditional methods were used to develop it, and the software was delivered as one big lump after 18 months of development. As the ship date drew closer, the developers began to pull the CS3 release together. There were many knocking pipes (i.e., defects or bugs). The developers didn't have time to fix them all, so they pulled the release together as best they could in the time frame and released it. Customer comments about CS3 included the following:

"But if you want an easy-to-use, user-friendly program for doing things with video, this is NOT it. There are things I expected it to do, and it didn't. Or I couldn't make it happen."[4]

* * *

" . . . this software is the notoriously bad encoder with memory leaks up the wazoo. If you try to encode a large movie file into mpeg2 premiere will more than likely crash on you due to bad memory management. The only solution so far is to simply restart the system and pray it wouldn't happen again."[5]

The next release, Premier Pro CS4, was meant to fix CS3's defects. CS4 was to increase the product's ease of use, stability, and speed, as well as halt memory leaks. Peter Green had heard about and decided that short-cycle development would allow Adobe to create complete increments of the total product with every Sprint. The increments would then add up into something that worked and that the customers would love. Peter also wanted to know the

---

[4] Review posted on Amazon.com on August 14, 2007.

[5] Review posted on Amazon.com on November 14, 2007.

real state of affairs every Sprint, so he had several of the teams that were working on CS4 try the Scrum process to see how it worked.

Adobe had over one hundred developers working on 18 Scrum Teams for this release. Everyone figured that integrating all of the increments from all 18 teams each Sprint would be too much work. They decided to wait until near the end of the release to integrate the increments. Just prior to the CS4 release date, the teams tried to integrate their individual pieces of software into one, integrated product. All the discrepancies and unresolved dependencies that precluded integration showed up as bugs and pieces of CS4 not working together. Figure 7.10 shows the slow increase in defects during the development prior to the attempted integration, and then the rapid spike in the number of defects. The developers heroically corrected as many as they could but still had to release the product late with harmful defects. The names of the developers who were hospitalized due to stress and overwork at Adobe are legend.

CS4 was released in September 2008, to poor industry reviews and negative customer feedback. Adobe had used Scrum to become more productive. However, only each individual team was more productive. The work of all the teams was not integrated and was not transparent. Potential integration

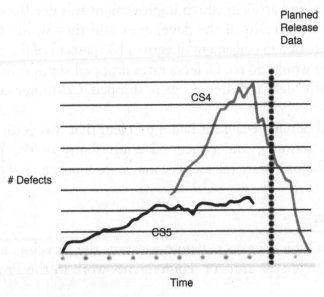

Figure 7.10   Defects in Adobe CS4 and CS5

problems were deferred for short-term productivity. Product quality, industry acceptance, timely release of new features, customer satisfaction, and employee morale and health deteriorated as a result. Something had to change.

Steve and Peter decided to use Scrum as widely as possible in CS5. They trained all the developers and program managers. Peter's new job was to teach and coach the teams so that they could build quality software with every Sprint. All increments from all the teams were integrated and tested at the end of each Sprint. Each Sprint essentially produced a release-level version of CS5. Figure 7.10 shows that the defects never got out of hand during this process. Much to everybody's surprise, the developers finished ahead of schedule. Unexpected defects and bugs from unintegrated increments weren't slowing them down. In the extra time at the end, they went back and fixed some of the problems left over from CS4 in their spare time. CS5 was released in April 2010, to glowing industry reviews and customer comments.

Peter was then asked to develop metrics that could be used to manage Scrum development at Adobe. He measured three dimensions. The first was employee satisfaction with Scrum during CS5, and the employees' belief that Scrum improved the way in which they built software. Adobe gave 200 developers from 25 teams a 50-question survey.[6] The results were analyzed by team and by question, and areas in which improvement was needed were identified. An impressive 80 percent of the developers said they would continue using Scrum even without a management directive; 100 percent of the best-performing teams said they would do so. Defects rates dropped significantly, and almost no products with "deferred" defects were shipped. Customer satisfaction rose significantly.

Adobe tried Scrum because it had a problem that was getting worse. With determination, training, and concerted effort many of the problems were addressed and their software releases became more timely and of higher quality.

Origins of Sin

Let's consider a typical project. Before we start, the Development Team estimates that there are 80 units of requirements work in the Product Backlog.

---

[6] Adobe administers this survey every six months.

You tell them that you hope to release this software in ten monthly Sprints. From habit, the Development Team divides 10 into 80, telling you that they have to complete 8 units of requirements work in every Sprint. They will select eight units of work per monthly Sprint, regardless of how much quality they have to leave out—how much work they have to skip in order to make the deadline.

In predictive development projects, the software organization estimated the requirements and predicted a date and cost. Its job was then to deliver accordingly. In a Scrum project, the development team delivers as much functionality in an increment as it can—at an organizationally defined fitness for purpose quality. You then can manage to a date by delivering all of the done functionality on that date, or you can choose the functionality you want and accept the date of its completion. Quality is no longer a variable.

Quality reduction has traditionally been a variable in software development. Systems are completed with minimum slippage if quality is reduced. However, quality reduction actually reduces productivity, increases cost, and causes more date slippage. Teams are burdened with additional work to fix the compounded defects and bugs. The only difference is that the reason for the slippage and cost increases is invisible to you.

Continuing our example, at the end of the tenth month, we expect to implement and use the software functionality. However, we have accumulated 48 units of undone work. We are not happy when we discover this. We think we should ask the developers to finish the undone work, to increase the percent finished for each Product Backlog item as soon as possible. However, we err if we demand that the developers do this "as soon as possible." This would usually require another six monthly Sprints (48 units of work divided by a probable velocity of 8). The remaining undone work is reflected in Figure 7.11 as the gap between work reported done and the accumulated undone and incomplete work.

Ultimately, the Development Team completes enough of the undone work so that the product "works." However, our customers soon tell us that the product is not fit for their consumption. At this point, the undone work becomes institutionalized in the software. It is technical debt that prevents people from effectively using the product. It also is the source of support calls and bug fixing that consumes our attention and money. Worst, it may cause our customers to look for better alternatives. We do not reap the benefits that we

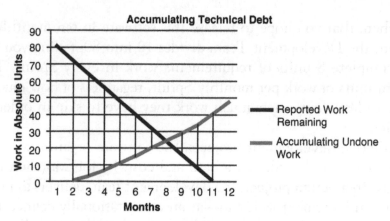

Figure 7.11 Technical Debt Accumulates as Work Is Done

expected. Technical debt progressively increases product fragility and shortens its expected life.

Consider a Development Team of three programmers and two quality engineers. They employ traditional, predictive practices. They write code and have somebody else, like quality control, see if it works. Any bugs or defects are detected and returned to the right programmer to fix. Time elapses between coding and the time that defects are detected and reported. During that time, the other programmers may have written more new software that is on top of or works with the defective software. The effort to fix the initial problem now takes longer. The effort to fix the software compounds across time. The compounding is identical to compound interest. Fixing problems as soon as they are created is critical. They must be detected and fixed when they occur. Then the developers can proceed without complicating the problem and compounding the effort to remediate it later.

Technical debt clouds transparency and renders decisions questionable. We measure our progress by comparing completed, usable pieces of software functionality against the remaining required pieces of functionality. We do not take into account unfinished work. Yet many software developers generate incomplete increments. Typically, when team members are asked why they only partially completed a number of product backlog requirements, rather than selecting and fully completing fewer, they say, "We didn't have time." We need to turn to our Scrum Master to ensure that this is not happening.

Software in 30 Days offers predictability, control of risk, and optimized value. The bedrock of these capabilities is frequent transparency. At least every 30 days, you will get to see what you have bought—in your terms. Many developers struggle with old habits and inadequate professional skills to create this transparency. There are many developers out there they have crossed this chasm. Your choice is to invest in your developers until they can also reliably develop software, or find another group of developers that can do so for you.

Summary

The Scrum software studio is a separate organization within your overall organization. The studio is not an effort to change the existing software development organization; rather, the studio is established so that anyone wanting to use Scrum to develop software can go there. The studio starts small and grows as it proves its value. The studio progressively becomes a place where software development is productive, high quality, and valuable. Risk is controlled, and projects are managed predictably. Testing and metrics are used to assess results empirically, to encourage continuous improvement.

The Scrum studio is a simple, fast way to start getting incremental, sustained improvement in software development. Scrum and the metrics it generates identify problem areas.

8

Scrum at the Enterprise Level

MANY ORGANIZATIONS ARE deciding to switch to Scrum. As with many other types of organizational transformation, the results depend on many factors. Some actual results are described in this chapter, along with the conditions that created each of them.

We have worked with many organizations, large and small, to help them transform and gain these benefits. The first publication about these efforts was "The Playbook for Achieving Enterprise Agility," produced through collaboration between Ken Schwaber and Rally Corporation in 2005. It was never published, but it was used frequently during Scrum rollouts. It can be found in Appendix 3.

Ken later wrote a book about enterprise adoption of Scrum in 2007, *The Enterprise and Scrum*.[1] He describes the strategies and tactics for doing so. The tactic of employing Scrum to manage the transformation itself is also described.

Profound but Transient Change

The type of adoption we have seen is usually extremely gratifying. The organization regularly puts out quality, valuable releases of software that are

---

[1] Ken Schwaber, *The Enterprise and Scrum* (Redmond, Washington: Microsoft Press, 2007).

welcomed by their customers. The development and product or customer organizations work well together to formulate and deliver new releases.

In the transformation to Scrum, the entire organization is in upheaval, working in controlled chaos for several years. Ultimately, software releases become better and better, the employees are happy to come to work, and customers begin to love working with the organization. However, the transformation is dependent on the senior executive who initiated it. Too often, this person is promoted out of the organization or recruited elsewhere before the other people who understand the new way of thinking and working are promoted throughout the organization, and before the transformation has been *anchored* into the organization. So when the senior executive leaves, the improvements unravel. The old culture, which was layered over but never rooted out, reasserts itself. The excellence and continuous improvement slowly decrease. The organization stays much, much better than it was before they started using Scrum, but it isn't what it could have been. People become careful. Within several years, the organization is not as bad as it was when it started, but it is not an agile Scrum organization either. Opportunity has been lost.

When we compare notes, we have found this to be true of almost every enterprise transformation that we know of and have been part of.

Primavera is an example of this type of transformation. Primavera produced a project management software package, TeamPlay, designed for the software development industry. All aspects of the waterfall process are automated in the product. In the early 2000s, Primavera struggled to complete new releases of TeamPlay. The releases were late, costly, incomplete, and unsatisfactory. In 2003, Primavera investigated using Scrum. Led by Bob Schatz, the executive in charge of development, the organization transformed itself. Product management, marketing, sales, personnel, support, and product development all became agile, opportunistic, and very competitive. The irony is that Primavera had to use an empirical process, Scrum, to build a predictive process tool, TeamPlay. The entire story is told on Bob's website.[2]

Bob left Primavera in 2005. His chief lieutenant, Ibrahim Abdelshafi, left Primavera shortly thereafter. The chief technology officer (CTO) and chief executive officer (CEO) of Primavera never really liked Scrum. They liked the results, but they did not like that it contradicted their product's usage. When

---

[2] www.agileinfusion.com/pdf/PrimaveraWhitePaper.pdf.

Bob and Ibrahim left, there was no senior management commitment to Scrum. Everyone still used a form of Scrum, but they used it less and less well. Transparency became opacity, predictability was lost, and so on. When Oracle acquired Primavera in 2008, it was better than it was before Scrum but it was no longer excellent. Significantly, the employees no longer looked forward to coming to work and doing great things.

Profound and Persistent Change

The most regaled and successful person in an organization is a senior executive who rolls out Scrum throughout the entire organization. This person knows what it takes to achieve significant organizational transformation. This person knows that cultural transformation has to be pervasive and complete in order to take root. When such a person describes the successes, he or she doesn't talk about what "I" did but about what other people did. John P. Kotter, a professor at the Harvard Business School and author of books on change, said, "When I go to talk with a CEO about organizational transformation, he usually has me meet with him and his staff. If his staff does the talking, I increase my assessment of their chance of success. If the CEO does all the talking, they don't stand a chance."[3]

True change must be achieved the old-fashioned way: with sweat equity. In order for transformation to occur, the entire organization must understand, create, and become a new culture. Even under the most compelling circumstances, enterprise transformation is profoundly difficult. Kotter, one of the most skillful change agents, estimates that this type of transformation requires five to seven years and that only 30 percent of organizations are successfully transformed. We have to look only at General Motors, Ford Motor Company, and Chrysler. In the face of scathing competition, they were unable to change for 40 years. Only now is change seeping in.

If you are interested in this type of change, we refer you to the experts. We would start with Kotter's excellent books, including *Leading Change* and *Our*

---

[3] John P. Kotter is a professor at the Harvard Business School and an author. He is regarded as an authority on leadership and change. Two of his more influential books are *Leading Change* (Boston: Harvard Business School Press, 1996) and *Our Iceberg Is Melting: Changing and Succeeding under Any Conditions* (New York St. Martin's Press, 2006).

Iceberg Is Melting. Then contact his organization or other organizations that specialize in organizational development.

Carbonite Transforms and Persists

Carbonite was founded in 2005 and went public in August, 2011. Carbonite's product provides automatic, online backup to personal computers, anytime and anywhere. Rob Rubin, Vice President for Development, has worked with Carbonite's founders, Jeff Flowers and David Friend, since the beginning. This was their sixth startup, so Rob counted on them providing vision and management competence, and Jeff and David counted on Rob's development-management skills. Yet by 2008, the primary Carbonite product was internally called "molasses." It took a long time to get a new release out.

In 2008, Carbonite had seven highly skilled developers, but they worked from home, not at the development area of Carbonite. There were seven product owners, each with his or her competing agenda, all of which were of highest priority. A new COO had just joined the organization and he had more ideas about what to do.

How Carbonite Broke the Mold

Rob heard a Scrum presentation at MIT in 2006. He really liked the idea that Scrum would give him things that he could measure. To Rob, a manager's job is first measurement, then action based on the measurement. Without measurement, it is impossible to manage. Rob wanted what Scrum provided: firm, transparent measurements of progress toward goals every 30 days and solid measurement of progress toward 30-day goals every day. Rob also believed that technology projects and products are difficult because their natures are complex and you cannot predict where they are going to fail. Their failures are random. The daily and 30-day information about progress or failure could be critical to his type of work.

Results

Rob trained his organization in Scrum in 2008. Since then, Carbonite has improved its release cycle while integrating worldwide acquisitions. At a recent luncheon, Rob and Jeff Flowers said that, without Scrum, Carbonite would not have been able to go public. Scrum gave it a standard process to use internally and to have its acquisitions use. Best of all, Scrum was not intrusive. If the acquired company had excellent development skills and processes, it kept them. It simply had to combine them with the Scrum model to provide the needed measurability and predictability.

Rob and Jeff believe in their employees. They use Scrum to create an environment in which the people working for Carbonite can be creative and best decide how to work. Scrum then provides the measurements that they use to focus on the very hard work of getting to be the best. All of them understand the problems and work together to solve them. In addition, Carbonite teams have a retrospective at the end of every Scrum Sprint. This retrospective is free-wheeling and intense. Anything that could make working at Carbonite better and produce better products is open for discussion. The discussions are heated but productive and are facilitated by Rob. The employees have bonded into a tight working team, even though they have expanded from seven to almost one hundred. They own and build their future. In 2011, the *Boston Business Journal* named Carbonite one of Boston's best places to work.[4]

Two Nonnegotiable Elements for Any Scrum Adoption

Two caveats to keep in mind when attempting to transform an organization are as follows:

Do Not Try to Change or Adapt Scrum

Scrum is not an approach or process that can be modified to fit the existing organizational culture; the culture must change to enable Scrum. Scrum exposes every cultural dysfunction that impedes developing software in the manner described in this book. For an organization, Scrum is the "canary in the coal mine."[5] If Scrum is not used as intended to create agile, transparent

---

[4] "Boston Business Journal Honors Carbonite as One of Boston's Best Places to Work." (2011, June 28). *Boston Business Journal*.

[5] Historically, coal miners placed canaries in the mines because canaries were more sensitive than people to carbon monoxide. When a canary stopped singing, it was time to get out of the mine.

development, problems remain invisible and continue to harm the enterprise. As such, a primary benefit of Scrum is lost.

Do Not Hesitate

Do not attempt to ease into organizational change. As in initiating anything worth doing, it is important that commitment be obvious, vigor be applied, and momentum be established at the onset. Once people begin to use Scrum, the most important impediments are more easily identified. There is a tendency in enterprises to overplan and to overthink. This is not the Scrum way. Scrum requires action, testing, evaluation, learning, elimination of impediments, and more action in order to create things of value for all concerned.

9

Enterprise Transformation:
Profound and Persistent Change

A SENIOR EXECUTIVE who led an organizational transformation to Scrum is a happy person. Just as happy are the organization's employees. They now have a great place to work and a great way to develop and market valuable software quickly—and they have achieved this through their own hard work.

The Enterprise Transformation Project

The path from initiation of an enterprise transformation project to realization of the vision consists of many activities, and it can take five or six years before the transition is complete—before profound and persistent change is embedded. Major changes will occur quickly, and benefits will occur within the first year. Significant competitive advantage will be reaped within two years. Even when the transformation is complete, continuous improvement—the heart of success—goes on forever.

You have used Scrum in one or more projects. You are convinced that you would like to use Scrum throughout the enterprise. To start, you should assess whether the type of change embodied in Scrum has enough value to be worth the cost of an organizational change project. You will gather the key people you will work with throughout the project so that they, as well as you, gain this certainty.

Once you decide to implement Scrum within your organization, a journey begins with a belief that the effort will be rewarded with a more effective software process and a more responsive and competitive company. It also recognizes that a significant amount of organizational change is now in the forecast.

Getting Ready

This section describes some typical examples of how you might implement Scrum throughout your organization; it can serve as a playbook, filled with sample techniques you can apply to accomplish the requisite change. The complete Playbook is included in Appendix 3 of this book.

The major activities of a transformation project are shown in Table 9.1, along with the average duration of each activity. Some activities may overlap.

Table 9.1   Major Activities of a Transformation Project

Activity	Required for Permanence	Average Duration
1. Start the transformation project.		1–3 months
1.1 Identify the benefits and urgency.	Yes	
1.2 Form a change team.		
1.3 Formulate a vision and strategy.	Yes	
2. Communicate the vision and strategy.	Yes	1–2 months
2.1 Address anxiety and resistance	Yes	
2.2 Create and execute communication tactics	Yes	
3. Expand throughout the organization.	Yes	1 month–5 years
4. Achieve impact.		2–6 months
5. Measure, assess, and consolidate gains.	Yes	1–5 years
5.1 Infiltrate	Yes	
5.2 Expand	Yes	
6. Embed, expand, and persist.	Yes	5–6 years

Activities that are mandatory to make the transition permanent are indicated by "Yes" in the "Required for Permanence" column.

Start the Transformation Project

The first play lays the groundwork for rest of the project. This play is laid out in Table 9.2. During it, you will learn what Scrum is and how to use it to improve and become agile. Key performance indicators for measuring agility and assessing its value are defined, perhaps building on those from the Scrum studio discussed in Chapter 6. The vision, goals, strategies, and tactics for the project are developed in this play, along with the budget and road map. The road map is very tentative and fully dependent on the energy and commitment of the transition team and the ability of the organization to change.

The energy for the transformation starts here, and the communication channels are initiated at this point.

Identify the Benefits and Urgency

Urgency arises from the organization's need to provide competitive services and products. If it cannot, its customers will go elsewhere. The message regarding the urgency needs to address two critical issues. The first is the need to remain competitive, just to stay in the game—to survive in the business. The second is the need to grow and prosper, to gain market share, and to have the most innovative products. The person or persons who believe that the transformation is urgent must present a compelling case for it. The story needs to be

Table 9.2 Start the Transformation Project

Activity	Required for Permanence	Average Duration
1. Start the transformation project.		1–3 months
1.1 Identify the benefits and urgency.	Yes	—
1.2 Form a change team.		—
1.3 Formulate a vision and strategy.	Yes	—

stated in as many ways possible: formal presentations are important, and financial models are required. Most important is a story of what will happen if transformation does occur. This story can be anecdotal, metaphorical, or a mocked-up model. But it needs to become part of the imagination of the organization's employees.

A transformation team that will drive this change is formed in this phase. The case for urgency is the sales tool for recruiting members to this team.

A statement of urgency could be as simple as this:

> We know we have problems using software to our advantage. Our projects are often late, don't meet our needs, and cost more than we can readily afford. This was acceptable only as long as there was no alternative. Now there is an alternative that is much better, called Scrum. Scrum is already used by some of our competitors. They are creating higher-quality products faster and with lower costs. They are gaining market share. If we don't learn to do what they are doing better than them, we are in trouble. Our revenues will decline, our customers will go to our competitors, and our employees will leave. We need to transform our organization.

Form a Change Team

The most senior executive who wants the transformation forms a new enterprise transformation project. He or she is the leader of the project and must be committed to the transformation. He forms a project team called the transformation team. This team is the heart of the transformation. It includes key executives who want the transformation to happen. Thought leaders throughout the organization who understand the urgency and want the transformation are also recruited.

This team will persist for the entire project. You may need to promote some of its members to critical transition positions within the organization as you proceed. This is also an opportunity to bring in new team members. The core transition team will consist of no more than seven to nine members. All of the members should be keenly interested in using Scrum to become agile; in increasing the professionalism in software development; in doing better, high-quality work; and in creating close, fruitful, and successful relationships with their customers.

Formulate a Vision and Strategy

The transformation team's job is to guide the organization from the current urgent situation to the envisioned state. It first develops a vision of what the organization will look like when the transformation is complete. By way of analogy, *Our Iceberg Is Melting* is a book that describes a colony of penguins living on an iceberg that is melting.[1] Unfortunately, the colony views the iceberg as its beloved home. The penguins must move but currently view themselves as living only on that iceberg. A new vision is created for the penguins as a migratory colony. The current iceberg is just their present home, but it is the colony that matters. They will continue as a colony when the iceberg melts; they just will live on another iceberg. This vision gives the colony something to hang onto, a context within which to view the upcoming changes. The new goal is to save the colony, and moving is the way to do that. Anxiety still exists about the transformation but not the about the future.

Every vision embraces the values that are needed to reach it. A vision statement could be similar to the following:

> Our organization benefits from the opportunities and challenges in our marketplace. We repeatedly create new, valuable, innovative offerings and products. We do so by engaging the intelligence and creativity of everyone in the organization. We make mistakes and learn from them. We are an open, transparent organization that is honest about itself, its strengths, its weaknesses, its current situation, and its opportunities. We are an organization of and for our employees. We value honest dialog and conflict, from which truth and opportunity arise.

This vision statement creates room for the Scrum values of transparency, empiricism, bottom-up intelligence, and knowledge creation.

During the initiation activity, the transformation team delineates the initial work in the transformation plan and creates the transformation backlog, For instance, the work to start communicating the next activity is identified, broken down into steps, clarified, and put into the transformation backlog. The work is ordered to optimize the value of the transformation and emerges

---

[1] J. P. Kotter, *Our Iceberg Is Melting: Changing and Succeeding under Any Conditions* (New York: St. Martin's Press, 2006), 62–71.

as time passes. Concrete projects are formulated from it. These projects are Sprints, and an increment of organizational change is the result of each Sprint. (The next chapter, "Scrumming Scrum," explains how the transformation team uses Scrum to manage the transformation.)

The outcomes from the initiation activities include a functioning transformation team, a statement of the urgency, a vision statement, a communication strategy, the transformation backlog, processes for proceeding, identification of doable transformation work for the next several months, and identification of metrics that will be used to track progress.

Communicate the Vision and Strategy

A clear communication strategy about the transformation has to be created. This play is laid out in Table 9.3. Regardless of how much communication occurs, it is never enough. As we work with organizations, we hear incredible things that are taken to be true. Lack of clarity is usually to blame. If people are worried that they don't know what to do or how to do it, communications are not effective.

Inadequate communication causes opacity, spin, and rumors. The message that the transformation team crafts and expands has to be clear. Communication about the need for the transformation has to be from the top down, the bottom up, and the middle out. Communication of the new vision and strategies needs to be done in many ways, including formal presentations, management announcements, working sessions, informal forums, gripe sessions, brown-bag lunches, one-on-one meetings with employees who have concerns, blogs, newsletters, documents, and members of management and the transformation team just walking around the organization. The communication has to be frequent and up to date. It has to be consistent.

Table 9.3 Communicate the Vision and Strategy

Activity	Required for Permanence	Average Duration
2. Communicate the vision and strategy	Yes	1–2 months
2.1 Address anxiety and resistance	Yes	
2.2 Create and execute tactics	Yes	

Communication includes behavior. Everything executives and managers say and do has to consistently support the transformation. Their behavior has to model the behavior that is expected of employees. If it doesn't, or if they say one thing and act otherwise, the transformation is damaged.

Address Anxiety and Resistance

People have seen books about Scrum on desks, and they have heard "inside information." The rumors start. The problem with rumors is that, because they are anonymous, people put their own opinions and worst fears into them. Rumors can freeze everyone in their tracks. They must be dispelled for any meaningful change to occur.

Everyone knows the existing culture of the organization: how managers act, how to get things done, how to get promoted, how to get a salary increase or bonus, how mistakes are handled, and so on. Even if they don't like the way things are at work, they are comfortable in knowing how things are. If people do not understand the vision for the future and where they fit into it, no matter how good it is, they will resist it. Employees at all levels need to know exactly what impact the proposed changes will have on them, their jobs, and their families' security. Many people will instinctively attempt to sandbag or water down any transformation unless they understand and feel secure about what is in it for them. If they do not understand what the proposed changes mean to them, personally, they will resist them now and in the future.

Resistance takes many forms. The most pernicious form is passive resistance. People do not object; they do not argue or disagree. They don't want to be identified as impediments, but they also don't want to change.

It is vitally important to get managers and other employees on board with the changes to come. These people are the organization's army. They know the business, the customers, the systems, and the products. They are the bedrock for change.

Create and Execute Tactics

The very first communication about the transformation should come from senior management to the entire organization. It should happen everywhere at once. The executives should describe the problem, the urgency, and the vision. They should explain the transformation team and the road map that it has laid out. They should describe all the ways in which people can communicate about this.

Managers and other employees should then go into smaller, departmental meetings for question-and-answer sessions. Handouts describing what the executives just communicated should be provided. When the employees leave these sessions, they should know how to communicate with one another, up and down the organization, to get their questions answered.

The transformation team also has to have a way of working with the people in the organization in order to learn what is going on in response to the formal announcements and the informal communications within the departments and overall organization.

Expand throughout the Organization

The first software development projects are initiated in play 3, in Table 9.4. Your organization already has some experience with Scrum, either from pilots (Chapter 3), individual projects (Chapter 4), or the Scrum studio (Chapter 5). These projects are part of a sustained introduction and use of Scrum by the development and product organizations. They are also causing change in all affected areas.

The transformation team has been developing a backlog of work that will transform the organization. Communication was at the top of the backlog. Now the team starts working on more items in the transformation backlog. It is critical at this time to include the following activities:

- *Teach and implement new vision, processes, and values:* People need to understand what is coming and why it is important to them. Exercise-based workshops help people understand better and also help solidify the communications.

Table 9.4   Expand throughout the Organization

Activity	Required for Permanence	Average Duration
3. Expand throughout the organization.	Yes	1 month–5 years

- *Remove known obstacles:* Start removing some of the well-known impediments. Everyone has a list of things that are in the way of productive software development. Change something that is currently required but hated. Onerous approval cycles usually are low-hanging fruit. Slate others for early removal. People will then start to believe that something different is happening—something that can benefit them.
- *Change structures and processes that undermine the change vision:* Some organizational structures and processes directly conflict with Scrum development practices. The roles of traditional managers, functional managers, and development managers must be reevaluated. Changing quality assurance practices might provide an early win.
- *Encourage risk taking and nontraditional ideas:* Encourage anything that helps move the organization forward. Assure managers that employees should be encouraged to explore, experiment, and learn from failures. Assure employees that initiative is encouraged and that learning the lessons that failures present is part of the process. Encourage everyone to learn from their mistakes and the mistakes of others, ensuring that one of the lessons is that failures are not punished.

Achieve Impact

Everyone in the organization needs to see progress toward the vision, as defined in play 4 in Table 9.5 Some early successes point the way and provide comfort. We advise the transformation team to select two software development projects that will form the bases for the early wins:

1. An enhancement project that builds new capabilities into an existing system that is no more than five years old.
2. A project to build a new system using modern technologies.

These projects each should be three to six months in duration. One of the projects, preferably the new development, should consist of 20 to 30 people,

Table 9.5 Achieve Impact

Activity	Required for Permanence	Average Duration
4. Achieve impact.		2–6 months

organized into three or four Scrum teams. The other project can consist of a single Scrum Team. Because almost any process works with an easy project, both projects should include difficult technologies and requirements; otherwise the assessments will be of limited value.

Have the teams execute the projects. They will build usable software for the organization. They also will uncover impediments that can be added to the transformation backlog. People will understand better how things will happen. The people who made the wins possible should be recognized and rewarded.

Measure, Assess, and Consolidate Gains

Play 5 as shown in Table 9.6 is the meat of the project. The three domains of development, change, and management interact to create progressively better products and an organization progressively structured to sustain these benefits. The transformation team and the rest of the organization really dig into transformation work during this activity.

The heart of Scrum is inspection and adaptation. Adaptation is how a new way of managing and developing software emerges. The transformation team continues to inspect what is going on, what the metrics show, and what impediments are being reported. The team prioritizes these needs in the transformation backlog. Sprints are based on this backlog, creating increments of organizational change and improvement that lead to the vision.

Infiltrate

Some people in the organization will completely understand and embrace Scrum and its underlying worldviews. This is the time to promote these people

Table 9.6 Measure, Assess, and Consolidate Gains

Activity	Required for Permanence	Average Duration
5. Measure, assess, and consolidate gains.	Yes	1–5 years
5.1 Infiltrate	Yes	
5.2 Expand	Yes	

into key influencing and management positions. They will keep the momentum going. Otherwise, the vision may be met for a short time but will unwind when the leaders inevitably leave the organization. By the end of the fourth year, new leadership should have been developed so that continuity of the effort is no longer an issue.

Expand

Use the credibility from early projects to change all systems, structures, and policies that don't align with the transformation vision. Expand Scrum to the rest of the development, product management, and internal customer organization functions. Have expansion occur project by project, with the uniqueness of each project contributing to the transformation.

Embed, Expand, and Persist

Anchoring the transformation means embedding the changes into the organization so that it acquires a new culture. Play 6 addresses this, as shown in Table 9.7. Any procedures, processes, habits, ways of doing things, or practices that were part of the organization's old culture are rooted out and replaced by new ways of doing things that support the transformation's vision.

Anchoring continues throughout the transformation process. It is not a goal but a practice that becomes part of the organization's continuous improvement and quest for excellence. Anything that doesn't work is replaced by something that works better. This leads to a knowledge-creating and learning organization.

As new ways of doing things are implemented, the connections between the vision, new behaviors, and organizational successes are reinforced through recognition, promotions, and bonuses. This cements everyone's understanding of what is valuable.

Table 9.7   Embed, Expand, and Persist

Activity	Required for Permanence	Average Duration
6. Embed, expand, and persist.	Yes	5–6 years

The organization will feel different. Opportunities will be taken advantage of quickly, and challenges will be addressed swiftly. The software systems and products used by the organization will be of significantly higher value. Development will be more productive and creative. People will be collaborating well together and sharing their enthusiasm and pleasure when they come to work.

Summary

An enterprise transformation project causes major upheaval in an organization. The transformation project must be led with commitment from the top and must employ excellent and consistent communication. The vision must be clear. The entire organization must participate and realize the benefits. The goal is a learning organization that continually renews and improves itself. The reward is excellence.

10

Scrumming Scrum

SCRUMMING SCRUM MEANS that the organization uses Scrum to implement Scrum, to execute the organizational transformation. To implement Scrum, an organization has to make two major changes. First, the software developers have to be formed into teams and taught how to create software using Scrum. Second, any impediments to the optimized creation and delivery of software must be removed. These impediments are discovered as the developers use Scrum. The first change will improve software delivery; the second will remedy impediments to productivity and return on investment. Both are challenging and require hard work. No matter what the intensity or commitment by management, the time required for these changes cannot be rushed, because they are a core part of the transformation project.

SeaChange International Scrums Itself with Scrum

SeaChange International is a worldwide leader in multiscreen video delivery products. Its technology is delivered through its partners, which include NBC, Comcast, Telus, PBS, SKY, Vodacom, Verizon, Cox, Time Warner Cable, and others that disseminate high-quality video. People from Digital Equipment Corporation started SeaChange in 1993.

119

Steve Davi, the head of SeaChange development, located in Boston, had to develop new functionality and new releases. He had to do this to keep SeaChange's products technologically advanced, and he also had to continually add new capabilities and features to stay on pace with the competition. That was adequate to stay in business. The challenge was to innovate and create new capabilities that the competition didn't have. Steve's strategy was to neutralize competitors' advantages while crushing them with SeaChange's advantages.

Steve faced many challenges. Many of the requirements were vague, and all urgent. The continuous introduction of new critical requirements was resulting in slips in release dates and unwanted features. Yet, Steve was aware that a changed requirement, even late in a release cycle, is a competitive advantage if you are able to act on it.

The sales organization at SeaChange arranged the sale of the next release, along with some additional requirements, to Verizon. It committed to delivery of a finished release in three months. Steve thought the release was impossible but, as is often the case, was told that he had to deliver. He worked his developers hard, including on weekends and nights. Within three months, they delivered about 90 percent of the release to Verizon. It was full of defects and performance problems. In the following six months, Steve frequently visited Verizon in Basking Ridge, New Jersey, to hear complaints, be berated for the product's poor quality, and promise that he would fix the problems.

Not surprisingly, Verizon didn't commercialize the new SeaChange software for six months after Steve's delivery. If Steve could have delivered just three months into that six-month buffer, his frequent visits to New Jersey would not have been required.

How SeaChange Broke the Mold

Steve knew that he needed some way to avoid repeating that experience. Also, SeaChange was rapidly expanding worldwide, acquiring new companies and integrating their products. Steve needed a way of managing products that worked, one that he could extend to the acquisitions.

People who embrace Scrum generally do so because they need to. If what they were doing worked, they wouldn't change. Change is difficult, traumatic, and risky. Only the desperate or visionary undertake it; generally, the problem must be perceived as greater than the difficulty and the risks. Furthermore, many managers are skilled in managing the status quo but not in managing change. Fortunately, one of Steve Davi's skills is change management. In 2005, he tried Scrum on one product: a new, web-based consumer product targeted at the social media marketplace. Scrum worked very well, and the product was delivered (frequently). Unfortunately, the product niche didn't become active until 2009, so the product was shelved. However, SeaChange became confident in using Scrum.

In fact, Steve used Scrum to manage the transition to Scrum! He created a small group of key managers and leads. The group created a list of things that needed to change, specific actions needed to create the changes, and problems they were encountering. The team worked from this list, creating substantive changes every 30 days. It met daily to assess progress and review unexpected problems. It communicated frequently what was happening and why, because change affects everyone and individuals want to know how it will affect them.

Management was charged with facilitating but not directing. Management's job changed from getting people to do what the plan said to doing everything they could to help their people meet the plan. "Resources" were creative people who were fully utilized. These and other changes in the corporate worldview were particularly difficult for middle managers, so they resisted the changes. One manager left because he couldn't work this way.

Another challenge occurred within the sales and marketing operation. Scrum calls for an ordered sequence of new and enhanced product capabilities. The plan changes frequently, but it is always visible. The developers work only from it. To make this process work, sales and marketing people had participated in creating the plan, knowing that their requirements and customer commitments would be prioritized vis-à-vis everyone's else's requirements. They had to agree based on the company's vision and product direction, rather than on personal desires or needs. This was a significant change. Sales and marketing personnel had to collaborate, pool ideas, and make decisions they would stick to.

As part of the change, SeaChange's staff and managers met frequently in retrospective sessions. They assessed what was happening and its effectiveness. They collaboratively devised and implemented ways to become more effective. A surprising change was in quality. Previously, the quality assurance operation was responsible for quality. Engineers would build as much functionality as they could into a product, and the quality assurance people would see if it worked. But in using Scrum, everyone is responsible for quality. Quality no longer is checked only at the end of a release. Each increment must be of high quality, with each increment progressively building on the quality of prior increments.

Results

SeaChange now uses Scrum worldwide. All acquired companies are required to adopt it. The acquisitions can retain all their successful practices, as was done at Carbonite. They use Scrum to surround these practices to create predictability, regularity, management information, and integration of everyone's work. Using Scrum, SeaChange has been able to keep up with and surge ahead of the competition. They have also been able to integrate new companies rapidly while quickly utilizing their products.

Iron Mountain Spreads Scrum

In Chapter 3, we discussed how Iron Mountain wrestled with dispersed developers and how Paul Luppino successfully resolved the problems. Scrum spread throughout the rest of the Iron Mountain development organization.

Paul was promoted and now works for the president of Iron Mountain, Harold Ebbighausen. He has applied Scrum principles to business management, and the six lines of business now have to report complete increments of work against their one-, three-, and six-month plans every 30 days. Management work, such as creating relationships, changing processes, working with customers to improve relationships, and solving organizational issues, is in a backlog, called a Transformation Product Backlog, which is described in more detail later in this chapter. Specific items must be completed within each Sprint. When something isn't completed, the entire management team works to understand the reason. Is the work intractable? Is the work item too big; does it need to be broken down into smaller pieces? Does the manager need help? The upcoming work is then reformulated for the next Sprint. Iron Mountain also has applied Scrum principles to general management. As both software development and organizations in general are very complex, Scrum has been effective in both applications.

Transformation Teams

Two Scrum Teams are employed during the transformation of the organization:

1. The transformation team, which uses Scrum to transform the organization to achieve the vision.
2. Rollout teams, which use Scrum for doing the actual work of transformation and causing change.

The Transformation Team

The most senior person leading the enterprise transformation project is the Product Owner of the transformation team. He or she can cut through organizational, departmental, and personal conflicts for the good of the entire enterprise. The Product Owner's stakeholders are everyone in the organization. A Scrum Master who is adept at facilitation and organizational development is also added to the team. The Scrum Master holds the transformation project together, keeps it sprinting to change the organization, and keeps it going using Scrum.

The transformation team can succeed only if its members work together collaboratively. If the individual successes of top executives are deemed more important than the team's success, the transformation will fail. Change cannot occur without collaboration and teamwork. An excellent primer for this type of teamwork is *The Five Dysfunctions of Teams* by Patrick Lencioni.[1]

Transformation Rollout Teams

The transformation team creates transformation rollout teams to effect the organizational change. These team select transformation Product Backlog work and transform the organization, bit by bit, through increments of change.

The transformation team creates these rollout teams as needed. They may either persist or be transient. Team members may come from management, may be Scrum Masters, or may be thought leaders from within the organization. Team members don't have to be full-time. They will be experts and

---

[1] P. Lencioni, *The Five Dysfunctions of a Team* (San Francisco: Jossey-Bass, 2002).

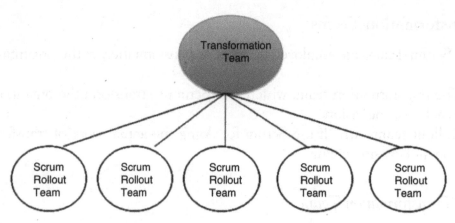

Figure 10.1   Transformation and Rollout Teams

leaders in the areas where the change will occur. Their availability and competence will dictate the pace of the transformation.

The rollout teams are different from the transformation team, which leads and directs the change (Figure 10.1). They are also different from the development Scrum teams, who build releases of software, increment by increment. The rollout teams build change.

Transformation Process

The enterprise transformation is complex. The transformation team manages the effort through Scrum, driving change Sprint by Sprint. The most important and possible changes are selected from the transformation Product Backlog by the transformation team and assigned to rollout teams. Transformation occurs, increment by increment.

Prior to Each Sprint The transformation team assesses the upcoming work in the transformation backlog prior to each Sprint. Rollout teams are identified based on the type of backlog. Members for each team are identified and recruited for the upcoming Sprints.

Sprint Planning Sprint Planning meetings last no more than one day. The rollout teams meet with the transformation Product Owner. The Product Owner discusses the upcoming changes and helps the rollout teams devise tactics and plans to create the changes. The rollout teams then forecast Product Backlog items for the Sprint.

Sprint The rollout teams Sprint to create an increment of change. The teams meet daily to assess progress and revise upcoming work, as necessary. Each team has a Scrum Master who reaches out to the transformation team Product Owner whenever impediments or obstacles are encountered.

Sprint Reviews A Sprint Review is held at the end of every Sprint. Tangible changes are demonstrated. The results of the change and the work of the change are assessed. The best work for the next transformation Sprint is assessed.

Sometimes rollout teams have nothing to demonstrate. This may mean that the wrong people were on the rollout team, that the members of the team weren't spending enough time on the problem, or that the problem was too difficult to solve as stated or in the current conditions. The remedy is to restructure the transformation Product Backlog or the team and try again.

Continue Sprinting Sprint by Sprint, the organization is transformed and transforms itself. The transformation team must be ruthless in seeking out new work. Self-congratulations and relaxation often occur before the change has been anchored. Then the change is impermanent, limited to the tenure of the people who led the change.

Summary

Scrum is a process for managing complex work. No work is more complex than changing an organization from one way of doing business to another. We've looked at how to use Scrum to do so. Scrum remains the same—just the work to be done in the backlog is different, as are the results.

Appendix 1: Terminology

Baseline	A line that is a base for measurement. In a burndown chart, it reflects the point in time when no requirements work remains to be done to complete the release.
Burndown chart	A chart that tracks the amount of requirements work remaining on a release across time, where time is measured in Sprints.
Daily Scrum meeting	The Daily Scrum is a 15-minute time-boxed event for the Development Team to synchronize activities and create a plan for the next 24 hours. This is done by inspecting the work since the last Daily Scrum and forecasting the work that could be done before the next one. The Daily Scrum is held at the same time and place each day to reduce complexity. During the meeting, each Development Team member explains: ■ What has been accomplished since the last meeting? ■ What will be done before the next meeting? ■ What obstacles are in the way?
Development Team	The Development Team consists of professionals who do the work of delivering a potentially releasable increment of "Done" product at the end of each Sprint. Only members of the Development Team create the increments.

Emergence	The way complex systems and patterns arise out of a multiplicity of relatively simple interactions. Emergence is central to the theories of integrative levels and of complex systems.
Empirical	Denotes information gained by means of observation or experimentation.
Forecast	A prediction based on experience of how much requirements effort in the Product Backlog can be transformed into an increment. This is not a guarantee.
Function point	A unit of measurement to express the amount of business functionality an information system provides to a user. The cost (in dollars or hours) of a single unit is calculated from past projects.
Increment	The increment is the sum of all the Product Backlog items completed during a Sprint and all previous Sprints. At the end of a Sprint, the new increment must be "done," which means it must be in useable condition and meet the Scrum Team's definition of "done." It must be in useable condition regardless of whether the Product Owner decides to actually release it.
Iteration	Iteration is the act of repeating a series of steps or processes, usually with the aim of approaching a desired goal or result. Each repetition of the process is also called an iteration, and the results of one iteration are used as the starting point for the next.
Iterative incremental, process	A way of developing a system or product through a sequence of iterations, each of which generates a complete increment of functionality that builds on all previous increments. Iterations continue until a goal is reached or value is optimized.
PRN	As necessary (from the Latin *pro re nata*, which means "take when needed").
Product Backlog	The Product Backlog is an ordered list of everything that might be needed in the product and is the single source of

requirements for any changes to be made to the product. The Product Owner is responsible for the Product Backlog, including its content, availability, and ordering.

Product Owner   The Product Owner is responsible for maximizing the value of the product and the work of the Development Team. How this is done may vary widely across organizations, Scrum Teams, and individuals.

Productivity   The number of units of business functionality that are developed for a specified amount of money (e.g., per $100,000 invested). Productivity is also called velocity.

Quality   The number of defects is counted starting on the day that the unit of functionality is given to the Product Owner and ending after three months of customer usage of the functionality.

Requirements   A singular documented physical and functional need that a particular product or service must be or perform. It is a statement that identifies a necessary attribute, capability, characteristic, or quality of a system for it to have value and utility to a user.

Scrum   An iterative, incremental process that employs empirical process control. Scrum is one of several agile processes.

Scrum Master   The Scrum Master is responsible for ensuring Scrum is understood and enacted. Scrum Masters do this by ensuring that the Scrum Team adheres to Scrum theory, practices, and rules. The Scrum Master is a servant-leader for the Scrum Team.

Scrum Team   The Scrum Team consists of a Product Owner, the Development Team, and a Scrum Master. Scrum Teams are self-organizing and cross functional.

Self-organization   The process where a structure or pattern appears in a system without a central authority or external element imposing it through planning.

Software developer   A person concerned with facets of the software development process. This person's work includes researching, designing, developing, and testing software.

Sprint	The heart of Scrum is a Sprint, a time-box of one month or less during which a "Done," useable, and potentially releasable product increment is created. Sprints have consistent durations throughout a development effort. A new Sprint starts immediately after the conclusion of the previous Sprint.
Sprint Backlog	The Sprint Backlog is the set of Product Backlog items selected for the Sprint, plus a plan for delivering the product Increment and realizing the Sprint Goal. The Sprint Backlog is a forecast by the Development Team, which determines what functionality will be in the next increment and the work needed to deliver that functionality.
	The Sprint Backlog defines the work the Development Team will perform to turn Product Backlog items into a "Done" increment. The Sprint Backlog makes visible all of the work that the Development Team identifies as necessary to meet the Sprint Goal.
Sprint Goal	The Sprint Goal gives the Development Team some flexibility regarding the functionality implemented within the Sprint.
	As the Development Team works, it keeps this goal in mind. In order to satisfy the Sprint Goal, it implements the functionality and technology. If the work turns out to be different than the Development Team expected, then they collaborate with the Product Owner to negotiate the scope of Sprint Backlog within the Sprint.
Sprint Planning Meeting	The work to be performed in the Sprint is planned at the Sprint Planning Meeting. This plan is created by the collaborative work of the entire Scrum Team.
	The Sprint Planning Meeting is time-boxed to eight hours for a one-month Sprint. For shorter Sprints, the event is proportionately shorter. For example, two-week Sprints have four-hour Sprint Planning Meetings.
	The Sprint Planning Meeting consists of two parts, each one being a time-box of one half of the Sprint Planning Meeting

duration. The two parts of the Sprint Planning Meeting answer the following questions, respectively:

- What will be delivered in the increment resulting from the upcoming Sprint?
- How will the work needed to deliver the increment be achieved?

Sprint Retrospective Meeting

The Sprint Retrospective is an opportunity for the Scrum Team to inspect itself and create a plan for improvements to be enacted during the next Sprint.

The Sprint Retrospective occurs after the Sprint Review and prior to the next Sprint Planning Meeting. This is a three-hour time-boxed meeting for one-month Sprints. Proportionately less time is allocated for shorter Sprints.

Sprint Review Meeting

A Sprint Review is held at the end of the Sprint to inspect the increment and adapt the Product Backlog if needed. During the Sprint Review, the Scrum Team and stakeholders collaborate about what was done in the Sprint. Based on that and any changes to the Product Backlog during the Sprint, attendees collaborate on the next things that could be done. This is an informal meeting, and the presentation of the increment is intended to elicit feedback and foster collaboration.

This is a four-hour time-boxed meeting for one-month Sprints. Proportionately less time is allocated for shorter Sprints.

Transparency

The nature of the increment as a completed piece of functionality, such that we can employ it to our purposes as well as determine our progress toward a vision or goal.

Trend (line)

A projection of velocity across time to forecast what might happen if everything in the future remains similar to what it was in the past.

Velocity

A measurement of how much business functionality is created during a period of time or for a unit of money.

Vision

A partially formed idea of something that functions in certain ways, can be used to do work, changes the world or workplace of its users in certain ways, and creates new value or presence in the world or marketplace that previously didn't exist in that form.

Waterfall   A sequential design process, often used in software development processes, in which progress is seen as flowing steadily downward (like a waterfall) through the phases of conception, initiation, analysis, design, construction, testing, production/implementation, and maintenance.

Appendix 2: The Scrum Guide

The Definitive Guide to Scrum: The Rules of the Game

Developed and sustained by Ken Schwaber and Jeff Sutherland

Table of Contents

Article I. Purpose of the Scrum Guide

Scrum is a framework for developing and sustaining complex products. This Guide contains the definition of Scrum. This definition consists of Scrum's roles, events, artifacts, and the rules that bind them together. Ken Schwaber and Jeff Sutherland developed Scrum; the Scrum Guide is written and provided by them. Together, they stand behind the Scrum Guide.

Article II. Scrum Overview

Scrum (n): A framework within which people can address complex adaptive problems, while productively and creatively delivering products of the highest possible value. Scrum is:

- Lightweight
- Simple to understand
- Extremely difficult to master

Scrum is a process framework that has been used to manage complex product development since the early 1990s. Scrum is not a process or a technique for building products; rather, it is a framework within which you can employ various processes and techniques. Scrum makes clear the relative efficacy of your product management and development practices so that you can improve.

Section 2.01 Scrum Framework

The Scrum framework consists of Scrum Teams and their associated roles, events, artifacts, and rules. Each component within the framework serves a specific purpose and is essential to Scrum's success and usage.

Specific strategies for using the Scrum framework vary and are described elsewhere.

The rules of Scrum bind together the events, roles, and artifacts, governing the relationships and interaction between them. The rules of Scrum are described throughout the body of this document.

Article III. Scrum Theory

Scrum is founded on empirical process control theory, or empiricism. Empiricism asserts that knowledge comes from experience *and* making decisions based on what is known. Scrum employs an iterative, incremental approach to optimize predictability and control risk.

Three pillars uphold every implementation of empirical process control: transparency, inspection, and adaptation.

(a) Transparency Significant aspects of the process must be visible to those responsible for the outcome. Transparency requires those aspects be defined by a common standard so observers share a common understanding of what is being seen.

For example:

- A common language referring to the process must be shared by all participants; and,
- A common definition of "Done"[1] must be shared by those performing the work and those accepting the work product.

(b) Inspection Scrum users must frequently inspect Scrum artifacts and progress toward a goal to detect undesirable variances. Their inspection should not be so frequent that inspection gets in the way of the work. Inspections are most beneficial when diligently performed by skilled inspectors at the point of work.

(c) Adaptation If an inspector determines that one or more aspects of a process deviate outside acceptable limits, and that the resulting product will be unacceptable, the process or the material being processed must be adjusted. An adjustment must be made as soon as possible to minimize further deviation.

Scrum prescribes four formal opportunities for inspection and adaptation, as described in the *Scrum Events* section of this document.

- Sprint Planning Meeting
- Daily Scrum

---

[1] See "Defination of "Done", p. 15.

- Sprint Review
- Sprint Retrospective

Article IV. Scrum

Scrum is a framework structured to support complex product development. Scrum consists of Scrum Teams and their associated roles, events, artifacts, and rules. Each component within the framework serves a specific purpose and is essential to Scrum's success and usage.

Article V. The Scrum Team

The Scrum Team consists of a Product Owner, the Development Team, and a Scrum Master. Scrum Teams are self-organizing and cross-functional. Self-organizing teams choose how best to accomplish their work, rather than being directed by others outside the team. Cross-functional teams have all competencies needed to accomplish the work without depending on others not part of the team. The team model in Scrum is designed to optimize flexibility, creativity, and productivity.

Scrum Teams deliver products iteratively and incrementally, maximizing opportunities for feedback. Incremental deliveries of "Done" product ensure a potentially useful version of working product is always available.

Section 5.01 The Product Owner

The Product Owner is responsible for maximizing the value of the product and the work of the Development Team. How this is done may vary widely across organizations, Scrum Teams, and individuals.

The Product Owner is the sole person responsible for managing the Product Backlog. Product Backlog management includes:

- Clearly expressing Product Backlog items;
- Ordering the items in the Product Backlog to best achieve goals and missions;
- Ensuring the value of the work the Development Team performs;

- Ensuring that the Product Backlog is visible, transparent, and clear to all, and shows what the Scrum Team will work on next; and,
- Ensuring the Development Team understands items in the Product Backlog to the level needed.

The Product Owner may do the above work, or have the Development Team do it. However, the Product Owner remains accountable.

The Product Owner is one person, not a committee. The Product Owner may represent the desires of a committee in the Product Backlog, but those wanting to change a backlog item's priority must convince the Product Owner.

For the Product Owner to succeed, the entire organization must respect his or her decisions. The Product Owner's decisions are visible in the content and ordering of the Product Backlog. No one is allowed to tell the Development Team to work from a different set of requirements, and the Development Team isn't allowed to act on what anyone else says.

Section 5.02 The Development Team

The Development Team consists of professionals who do the work of delivering a potentially releasable Increment of "Done" product at the end of each Sprint. Only members of the Development Team create the Increment.

Development Teams are structured and empowered by the organization to organize and manage their own work. The resulting synergy optimizes the Development Team's overall efficiency and effectiveness. Development Teams have the following characteristics:

- They are self-organizing. No one (not even the Scrum Master) tells the Development Team how to turn Product Backlog into Increments of potentially releasable functionality;
- Development Teams are cross-functional, with all of the skills as a team necessary to create a product Increment;
- Scrum recognizes no titles for Development Team members other than Developer, regardless of the work being performed by the person; there are no exceptions to this rule;

- Individual Development Team members may have specialized skills and areas of focus, but accountability belongs to the Development Team as a whole; and,
- Development Teams do not contain sub-teams dedicated to particular domains like testing or business analysis.

(a) Development Team Size Optimal Development Team size is small enough to remain nimble and large enough to complete significant work. Fewer than three Development Team members decreases interaction and results in smaller productivity gains. Smaller Development Teams may encounter skill constraints during the Sprint, causing the Development Team to be unable to deliver a potentially releasable Increment. Having more than nine members requires too much coordination. Large Development Teams generate too much complexity for an empirical process to manage. The Product Owner and Scrum Master roles are not included in this count unless they are also executing the work of the Sprint Backlog.

Section 5.03 The Scrum Master

The Scrum Master is responsible for ensuring Scrum is understood and enacted. Scrum Masters do this by ensuring that the Scrum Team adheres to Scrum theory, practices, and rules. The Scrum Master is a servant-leader for the Scrum Team.

The Scrum Master helps those outside the Scrum Team understand which of their interactions with the Scrum Team are helpful and which aren't. The Scrum Master helps everyone change these interactions to maximize the value created by the Scrum Team.

(a) Scrum Master Service to the Product Owner The Scrum Master serves the Product Owner in several ways, including:

- Finding techniques for effective Product Backlog management;
- Clearly communicating vision, goals, and Product Backlog items to the Development Team;
- Teaching the Scrum Team to create clear and concise Product Backlog items;

- Understanding long-term product planning in an empirical environment;
- Understanding and practicing agility; and,
- Facilitating Scrum events as requested or needed.

(b) Scrum Master Service to the Development Team The Scrum Master serves the Development Team in several ways, including:

- Coaching the Development Team in self-organization and cross-functionality;
- Teaching and leading the Development Team to create high-value products;
- Removing impediments to the Development Team's progress;
- Facilitating Scrum events as requested or needed; and,
- Coaching the Development Team in organizational environments in which Scrum is not yet fully adopted and understood.

(c) Scrum Master Service to the Organization The Scrum Master serves the organization in several ways, including:

- Leading and coaching the organization in its Scrum adoption;
- Planning Scrum implementations within the organization;
- Helping employees and stakeholders understand and enact Scrum and empirical product development;
- Causing change that increases the productivity of the Scrum Team; and,
- Working with other Scrum Masters to increase the effectiveness of the application of Scrum in the organization.

Article VI. Scrum Events

Prescribed events are used in Scrum to create regularity and to minimize the need for meetings not defined in Scrum. Scrum uses time-boxed events, such that every event has a maximum duration. This ensures an appropriate amount of time is spent planning without allowing waste in the planning process.

Other than the Sprint itself, which is a container for all other events, each event in Scrum is a formal opportunity to inspect and adapt something. These events are specifically designed to enable critical transparency and inspection. Failure to include any of these events results in reduced transparency and is a lost opportunity to inspect and adapt.

Section 6.01 The Sprint

The heart of Scrum is a Sprint, a time-box of one month or less during which a "Done", useable, and potentially releasable product Increment is created. Sprints have consistent durations throughout a development effort. A new Sprint starts immediately after the conclusion of the previous Sprint.

- Sprints contain and consist of the Sprint Planning Meeting, Daily Scrums, the development work, the Sprint Review, and the Sprint Retrospective.

  During the Sprint:

- No changes are made that would affect the Sprint Goal;
- Development Team composition remains constant;
- Quality goals do not decrease; and,
- Scope may be clarified and re-negotiated between the Product Owner and Development Team as more is learned.

Each Sprint may be considered a project with no more than a one-month horizon. Like projects, Sprints are used to accomplish something. Each Sprint has a definition of what is to be built, a design and flexible plan that will guide building it, the work, and the resultant product.

Sprints are limited to one calendar month. When a Sprint's horizon is too long the definition of what is being built may change, complexity may rise, and risk may increase. Sprints enable predictability by ensuring inspection and adaptation of progress toward a goal at least every calendar month. Sprints also limit risk to one calendar month of cost.

(a) Cancelling a Sprint A Sprint can be cancelled before the Sprint time-box is over. Only the Product Owner has the authority to cancel the Sprint, although he or she may do so under influence from the stakeholders, the Development Team, or the Scrum Master.

A Sprint would be cancelled if the Sprint Goal becomes obsolete. This might occur if the company changes direction or if market or technology conditions change. In general, a Sprint should be cancelled if it no longer makes sense given the circumstances. But, due to the short duration of Sprints, cancellation rarely makes sense.

When a Sprint is cancelled, any completed and "Done" Product Backlog Items are reviewed. If part of the work is potentially releasable, the Product Owner typically accepts it. All incomplete Product Backlog Items are re-estimated and put back on the Product Backlog. The work done on them depreciates quickly and must be frequently re-estimated.

Sprint cancellations consume resources, since everyone has to regroup in another Sprint Planning Meeting to start another Sprint. Sprint cancellations are often traumatic to the Scrum Team, and are very uncommon.

Section 6.02 Sprint Planning Meeting

The work to be performed in the Sprint is planned at the Sprint Planning Meeting. This plan is created by the collaborative work of the entire Scrum Team.

The Sprint Planning Meeting is time-boxed to eight hours for a one-month Sprint. For shorter Sprints, the event is proportionately shorter. For example, two-week Sprints have four-hour Sprint Planning Meetings.

The Sprint Planning Meeting consists of two parts, each one being a time-box of one half of the Sprint Planning Meeting duration. The two parts of the Sprint Planning Meeting answer the following questions, respectively:

- What will be delivered in the Increment resulting from the upcoming Sprint?
- How will the work needed to deliver the Increment be achieved?

(a) Part One: What will be done this Sprint? In this part, the Development Team works to forecast the functionality that will be developed during the Sprint. The Product Owner presents ordered Product Backlog items to the Development Team and the entire Scrum Team collaborates on understanding the work of the Sprint.

The input to this meeting is the Product Backlog, the latest product Increment, projected capacity of the Development Team during the Sprint, and past performance of the Development Team. The number of items selected from the Product Backlog for the Sprint is solely up to the Development Team. Only the Development Team can assess what it can accomplish over the upcoming Sprint.

After the Development Team forecasts the Product Backlog items it will deliver in the Sprint, the Scrum Team crafts a Sprint Goal. The Sprint Goal is an objective that will be met within the Sprint through the implementation of the Product Backlog, and it provides guidance to the Development Team on why it is building the Increment.

(b) Part Two: How will the chosen work get done? Having selected the work of the Sprint, the Development Team decides how it will build this functionality into a "Done" product Increment during the Sprint. The Product Backlog items selected for this Sprint plus the plan for delivering them is called the Sprint Backlog.

The Development Team usually starts by designing the system and the work needed to convert the Product Backlog into a working product Increment. Work may be of varying size, or estimated effort. However, enough work is planned during the Sprint Planning Meeting for the Development Team to forecast what it believes it can do in the upcoming Sprint. Work planned for the first days of the Sprint by the Development Team is decomposed to units of one day or less by the end of this meeting. The Development Team self-organizes to undertake the work in the Sprint Backlog, both during the Sprint Planning Meeting and as needed throughout the Sprint.

The Product Owner may be present during the second part of the Sprint Planning Meeting to clarify the selected Product Backlog items and to help make trade-offs. If the Development Team determines it has too much or too little work, it may renegotiate the Sprint Backlog items with the Product Owner. The Development Team may also invite other people to attend in order to provide technical or domain advice.

By the end of the Sprint Planning Meeting, the Development Team should be able to explain to the Product Owner and Scrum Master how it intends to work as a self-organizing team to accomplish the Sprint Goal and create the anticipated Increment.

(c) Sprint Goal The Sprint Goal gives the Development Team some flexibility regarding the functionality implemented within the Sprint.

As the Development Team works, it keeps this goal in mind. In order to satisfy the Sprint Goal, it implements the functionality and technology. If the work turns out to be different than the Development Team expected, then they collaborate with the Product Owner to negotiate the scope of Sprint Backlog within the Sprint.

The Sprint Goal may be a milestone in the larger purpose of the product roadmap.

Section 6.03 *Daily Scrum*

The Daily Scrum is a 15-minute time-boxed event for the Development Team to synchronize activities and create a plan for the next 24 hours. This is done by inspecting the work since the last Daily Scrum and forecasting the work that could be done before the next one.

The Daily Scrum is held at the same time and place each day to reduce complexity. During the meeting, each Development Team member explains:

- What has been accomplished since the last meeting?
- What will be done before the next meeting?
- What obstacles are in the way?

The Development Team uses the Daily Scrum to assess progress toward the Sprint Goal and to assess how progress is trending toward completing the work in the Sprint Backlog. The Daily Scrum optimizes the probability that the Development Team will meet the Sprint Goal. The Development Team often meets immediately after the Daily Scrum to re-plan the rest of the Sprint's work. Every day, the Development Team should be able to explain to the Product Owner and Scrum Master how it intends to work together as a self-organizing team to accomplish the goal and create the anticipated Increment in the remainder of the Sprint.

The Scrum Master ensures that the Development Team has the meeting, but the Development Team is responsible for conducting the Daily Scrum. The Scrum Master teaches the Development Team to keep the Daily Scrum within the 15-minute time-box.

The Scrum Master enforces the rule that only Development Team members participate in the Daily Scrum. The Daily Scrum is not a status meeting, and is for the people transforming the Product Backlog items into an Increment.

Daily Scrums improve communications, eliminate other meetings, identify and remove impediments to development, highlight and promote quick decision-making, and improve the Development Team's level of project knowledge. This is a key inspect and adapt meeting.

Section 6.04 Sprint Review

A Sprint Review is held at the end of the Sprint to inspect the Increment and adapt the Product Backlog if needed. During the Sprint Review, the Scrum Team and stakeholders collaborate about what was done in the Sprint. Based on that and any changes to the Product Backlog during the Sprint, attendees collaborate on the next things that could be done. This is an informal meeting, and the presentation of the Increment is intended to elicit feedback and foster collaboration.

This is a four-hour time-boxed meeting for one-month Sprints. Proportionately less time is allocated for shorter Sprints. For example, two-week Sprints have two-hour Sprint Reviews.

The Sprint Review includes the following elements:

- The Product Owner identifies what has been "Done" and what has not been "Done";
- The Development Team discusses what went well during the Sprint, what problems it ran into, and how those problems were solved;
- The Development Team demonstrates the work that it has "Done" and answers questions about the Increment;
- The Product Owner discusses the Product Backlog as it stands. He or she projects likely completion dates based on progress to date; and,
- The entire group collaborates on what to do next, so that the Sprint Review provides valuable input to subsequent Sprint Planning Meetings.

The result of the Sprint Review is a revised Product Backlog that defines the probable Product Backlog items for the next Sprint. The Product Backlog may also be adjusted overall to meet new opportunities.

Section 6.05 Sprint Retrospective

The Sprint Retrospective is an opportunity for the Scrum Team to inspect itself and create a plan for improvements to be enacted during the next Sprint.

The Sprint Retrospective occurs after the Sprint Review and prior to the next Sprint Planning Meeting. This is a three-hour time-boxed meeting for one-month Sprints. Proportionately less time is allocated for shorter Sprints.

The purpose of the Sprint Retrospective is to:

- Inspect how the last Sprint went with regards to people, relationships, process, and tools;
- Identify and order the major items that went well and potential improvements; and,
- Create a plan for implementing improvements to the way the Scrum Team does its work.

The Scrum Master encourages the Scrum Team to improve, within the Scrum process framework, its development process and practices to make it more effective and enjoyable for the next Sprint. During each Sprint Retrospective, the Scrum Team plans ways to increase product quality by adapting the Definition of "Done" as appropriate.

By the end of the Sprint Retrospective, the Scrum Team should have identified improvements that it will implement in the next Sprint. Implementing these improvements in the next Sprint is the adaptation to the inspection of the Scrum Team itself. Although improvements may be implemented at any time, the Sprint Retrospective provides a formal opportunity to focus on inspection and adaptation.

Article VII. Scrum Artifacts

Scrum's artifacts represent work or value in various ways that are useful in providing transparency and opportunities for inspection and adaptation. Artifacts defined by Scrum are specifically designed to maximize transparency of key information needed to ensure Scrum Teams are successful in delivering a "Done" Increment.

Section 7.01 Product Backlog

The Product Backlog is an ordered list of everything that might be needed in the product and is the single source of requirements for any changes to be made to the product. The Product Owner is responsible for the Product Backlog, including its content, availability, and ordering.

A Product Backlog is never complete. The earliest development of it only lays out the initially known and best-understood requirements. The Product Backlog evolves as the product and the environment in which it will be used evolves. The Product Backlog is dynamic; it constantly changes to identify what the product needs to be appropriate, competitive, and useful. As long as a product exists, its Product Backlog also exists.

The Product Backlog lists all features, functions, requirements, enhancements, and fixes that constitute the changes to be made to the product in future releases. Product Backlog items have the attributes of a description, order, and estimate.

The Product Backlog is often ordered by value, risk, priority, and necessity. Top-ordered Product Backlog items drive immediate development activities. The higher the order, the more a Product Backlog item has been considered, and the more consensus exists regarding it and its value.

Higher ordered Product Backlog items are clearer and more detailed than lower ordered ones. More precise estimates are made based on the greater clarity and increased detail; the lower the order, the less detail. Product Backlog items that will occupy the Development Team for the upcoming Sprint are fine-grained, having been decomposed so that any one item can be "Done" within the Sprint time-box. Product Backlog items that can be "Done" by the Development Team within one Sprint are deemed "ready" or "actionable" for selection in a Sprint Planning Meeting.

As a product is used and gains value, and the marketplace provides feedback, the Product Backlog becomes a larger and more exhaustive list. Requirements never stop changing, so a Product Backlog is a living artifact. Changes in business requirements, market conditions, or technology may cause changes in the Product Backlog.

Multiple Scrum Teams often work together on the same product. One Product Backlog is used to describe the upcoming work on the product. A Product Backlog attribute that groups items is then employed.

Product Backlog grooming is the act of adding detail, estimates, and order to items in the Product Backlog. This is an ongoing process in which the Product Owner and the Development Team collaborate on the details of Product Backlog items. During Product Backlog grooming, items are reviewed and revised. However, they can be updated at any time by the Product Owner or at the Product Owner's discretion.

Grooming is a part-time activity during a Sprint between the Product Owner and the Development Team. Often the Development Team has the domain knowledge to perform grooming itself. How and when grooming is done is decided by the Scrum Team. Grooming usually consumes no more than 10% of the capacity of the Development Team.

The Development Team is responsible for all estimates. The Product Owner may influence the Development Team by helping understand and select trade-offs, but the people who will perform the work make the final estimate.

(a) Monitoring Progress Toward a Goal At any point in time, the total work remaining to reach a goal can be summed. The Product Owner tracks this total work remaining at least for every Sprint Review. The Product Owner compares this amount with work remaining at previous Sprint Reviews to assess progress toward completing projected work by the desired time for the goal. This information is made transparent to all stakeholders.

Various trend burndown, burnup and other projective practices have been used to forecast progress. These have proven useful. However, these do not replace the importance of empiricism. In complex environments, what will happen is unknown. Only what has happened may be used for forward-looking decision-making.

Section 7.02 Sprint Backlog

The Sprint Backlog is the set of Product Backlog items selected for the Sprint plus a plan for delivering the product Increment and realizing the Sprint Goal. The Sprint Backlog is a forecast by the Development Team about what functionality will be in the next Increment and the work needed to deliver that functionality.

The Sprint Backlog defines the work the Development Team will perform to turn Product Backlog items into a "Done" Increment. The Sprint Backlog makes visible all of the work that the Development Team identifies as necessary to meet the Sprint Goal.

The Sprint Backlog is a plan with enough detail that changes in progress can be understood in the Daily Scrum. The Development Team modifies Sprint Backlog throughout the Sprint, and the Sprint Backlog emerges during the Sprint. This emergence occurs as the Development Team works through the plan and learns more about the work needed to achieve the Sprint Goal.

As new work is required, the Development Team adds it to the Sprint Backlog. As work is performed or completed, the estimated remaining work is updated. When elements of the plan are deemed unnecessary, they are removed. Only the Development Team can change its Sprint Backlog during a Sprint. The Sprint Backlog is a highly visible, real-time picture of the work that the Development Team plans to accomplish during the Sprint, and it belongs solely to the Development Team.

(a) **Monitoring Sprint Progress** At any point in time in a Sprint, the total work remaining in the Sprint Backlog items can be summed. The Development Team tracks this total work remaining at least for every Daily Scrum. The Development Team tracks these sums daily and projects the likelihood of achieving the Sprint Goal. By tracking the remaining work throughout the Sprint, the Development Team can manage its progress.

Scrum does not consider the time spent working on Sprint Backlog Items. The work remaining and date are the only variables of interest.

Section 7.03 Increment

The Increment is the sum of all the Product Backlog items completed during a Sprint and all previous Sprints. At the end of a Sprint, the new Increment must be "Done," which means it must be in useable condition and meet the Scrum Team's Definition of "Done." It must be in useable condition regardless of whether the Product Owner decides to actually release it.

Article VIII. Definition of "Done"

When the Product Backlog item or an Increment is described as "Done", everyone must understand what "Done" means. Although this varies significantly per Scrum Team, members must have a shared understanding of what it means for work to be complete, to ensure transparency. This is the "Definition of Done" for the Scrum Team and is used to assess when work is complete on the product Increment.

The same definition guides the Development Team in knowing how many Product Backlog items it can select during a Sprint Planning Meeting. The purpose of each Sprint is to deliver Increments of potentially releasable functionality that adhere to the Scrum Team's current Definition of "Done."

Development Teams deliver an Increment of product functionality every Sprint. This Increment is useable, so a Product Owner may choose to immediately release it. Each Increment is additive to all prior Increments and thoroughly tested, ensuring that all Increments work together.

As Scrum Teams mature, it is expected that their Definition of "Done" will expand to include more stringent criteria for higher quality.

Article IX. Conclusion

Scrum is free and offered in this guide. Scrum's roles, artifacts, events, and rules are immutable and although implementing only parts of Scrum is possible, the result is not Scrum. Scrum exists only in its entirety and functions well as a container for other techniques, methodologies, and practices.

Article X. Acknowledgements

Section 10.01 People

Of the thousands of people who have contributed to Scrum, we should single out those who were instrumental in its first ten years. First there was Jeff Sutherland, working with Jeff McKenna, and Ken Schwaber, working with Mike Smith and Chris Martin. Many others contributed in the ensuing years and without their help Scrum would not be refined as it is today. David Starr provided key insights and editorial skills in formulating this version of the Scrum Guide.

Section 10.02 History

Ken Schwaber and Jeff Sutherland first co-presented Scrum at the OOPSLA conference in 1995. This presentation essentially documented the learning that Ken and Jeff had over the previous few years applying Scrum.

The history of Scrum is already considered long. To honor the first places where it was tried and refined, we recognize Individual, Inc., Fidelity Investments, and IDX (now GE Medical).

The Scrum Guide documents Scrum as developed and sustained for twenty-plus years by Jeff Sutherland and Ken Schwaber. Other sources provide you with patterns, processes, and insights about how the practices, facilitations, and tools that complement the Scrum framework. These optimize productivity, value, creativity, and pride.

Appendix 3: A Playbook for Achieving Enterprise Agility

Employed Since 2005

Table of Contents

1.1 Introduction

The pressures of a truly global economy cause today's business to increasingly rely on their ability to produce *software* as a key competitive advantage. Whether it's software for managing manufacturing and customer delivery processes or software improving the efficiency of day-to-day activities, software touches virtually every facet of today's business.

And yet, many CXOs find their software development practices remain little changed from the 1980s. Reliance on prescriptive, plan-based, waterfall-like methods is common despite mountains of evidence that these practices often fail to deliver real value in a timely fashion, and so hamper the company's responsiveness to fast-changing customer requirements and market conditions. And it's not getting easier.

Today's IT organizations must also effectively coordinate globally distributed software development teams while re-factoring legacy applications into more flexible, service oriented architectures. Clearly, we need a new approach for managing and developing software to remain competitive.

To address these challenges, a number of more agile and adaptive software development techniques are being adopted which allow organizations to more quickly deliver high value software. *Scrum* is one such proven method that has been widely adopted by many software organizations. This whitepaper describes how a CXO or other executive can implement Scrum on an organization-wide basis, including scaling across larger applications and teams of teams – the challenges he or she will face as well as the rewards – and

> Managing distributed organizations and effectively migrating to service oriented architectures demand a new software development approach

provides a *playbook* for adopting Scrum in enterprises where software, and lots of it, is the key to competitive success in the marketplace.

This is a "playbook" of ideas about implementing Scrum within an enterprise. It's a playbook rather than a manual because each organization is unique. Scrum's implementation in one enterprise will be different from its implementation in another. The types of impediments, things that need changing, the difficulty of change, and the people who will be doing the changing are different, so the timetables, the priorities, and the effort will be different as well.

1.2 Overview of Scrum and Software Agility

On the surface, Scrum is a very simple process: a software management technique that has a relatively small set of interrelated practices and rules, is not overly prescriptive, can be learned quickly and is able to produce productivity gains almost immediately.

Scrum naturally focuses an entire organization on building successful products. It delivers useful features at regular intervals as requirements, architecture, and design emerge, even when using unstable technologies. You can implement Scrum at the beginning of a project or in the middle of a project, and Scrum has saved many development efforts that were in trouble.

Scrum works because it optimizes the development environment, reduces organizational overhead, and closely synchronizes market requirements with early feature delivery. Based in modern process control theory, Scrum produces the best possible software given the available resources, acceptable quality levels, and required release dates.

At its core, Scrum is an iterative, incremental process for developing any product or managing any work that produces a potentially shippable set of functionality at the end of each iteration. Scrum's attributes are:

- Scrum is a tool that can be used to achieve agility.
- Scrum is an agile process to manage and control development work.
- Scrum is a wrapper for existing engineering practices.
- Scrum is a team-based approach to developing systems when requirements are changing rapidly.
- Scrum controls the chaos of conflicting interests and needs.
- Scrum improves communication and maximizes cooperation.
- Scrum detects and removes anything that gets in the way of developing and delivering products.
- Scrum is a way to maximize productivity.
- Scrum scales from single projects to entire organizations, and has managed development for multiple interrelated products and projects with over a thousand team members.
- Scrum is a way for everyone to feel good about their job, their contributions, and know they have done the very best they possibly could.

While describing Scrum practices in detail is outside the scope of this whitepaper (see Schwaber 2004 and Schwaber 2002), the method is characterized by the production of a *Product Backlog* where requested features are organized by their priority (Figure A3.1). A *Product Owner* is responsible for approving changes to the product backlog. Implementation occurs in roughly 30-day iterations called *Sprints*, which focus on the top priorities in the Product Backlog. The goal of each Sprint is to deliver a potentially shippable product increment. During the Sprint, checkpoints are observed in a daily "Scrum" meeting, which communicates the progress and activities within the team and shares issues that may be "blocking" progress for an individual or the team. This allows the Scrum Master to determine progress against the Sprint commitments and advise on midcourse corrections to assure successful completion of the Sprint. The overall process flow is shown in Figure A3.1.

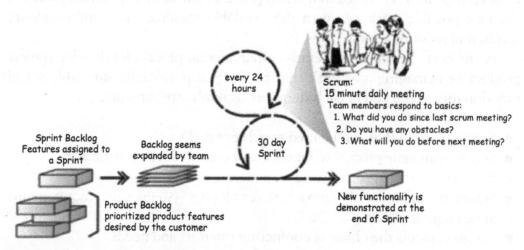

Figure A3.1   An Empirical Process Model for Scrum

1.2.1 Scrum Principles

While those are some of the mechanics of Scrum, more importantly, the CXO should understand that Scrum is guided by a few key principles:

- The belief that effective software development is best implemented via an *empirical* rather than *planned* process;

- The belief that, once organizational impediments are removed, a self organizing and self managing team will naturally deliver better software than would otherwise be the case;
- The premise that you can deliver the most valuable software within a prescribed time and budget, and yet you *cannot* definitively predict the exact functionality of what a team will deliver.

Scrum's assertion is that recognizing these key principles frees an organization from many of the constraints that prevent effective software development. However, CXOs must also recognize that these key principles imply potentially significant *change* to the organization that chooses to adopt them. Since these principles form the underlying basis of Scrum, each merits some additional discussion.

1.1.2.1 Adopting an Empirical vs. Planned Process Scrum believes that most systems development today has an incorrect philosophical basis, that is, through more and better planning we can achieve more predictable, higher quality results. Scrum recognizes that the applications development process is an unpredictable and extraordinary complicated process (think hundreds of thousands of manually created lines of code) whose value can only be measured empirically. After all, the application under development has likely not been developed by any team anywhere, ever, much less by your team in your context, so cookbook, step-by-step planning approaches cannot effectively address the inherent unpredictability.

Scrum defines the systems development process as a loose set of activities that combines known, workable tools and techniques with an empowered team that is tightly coupled to the Customer/Product Owner. Since many of these activities are loose, controls are applied – such as constant inspection and demonstration –to manage the risk and provide real time, empirical evidence of the state of the project at every point in time.

The Scrum tradeoff is simple:

Know where you are every day with Scrum

- or -

Think you know where you are on your well-formed plan and discover that you are very wrong, very much later

1.2.1.2 Eliminate the Impediments So the Team Can Do its Job Over the years, a company's organizational processes and software development practices typically gain weight until building software is often quite a difficult endeavor. When Scrum is implemented, these "organizational impediments" to effective software delivery become quite obvious, for they get in the way of the team's ability to deliver on the rapid iterative, incremental nature of Scrum. Removing or changing these processes and practices may show that a major change project must be initiated, driven and monitored by the CXO or executive champion (more on this topic later).

Moreover, in Scrum, *the team is the thing*. After all, they are the ones who actually design, develop and deliver the application, so optimizing their performance by eliminating obstacles optimizes the business's performance in delivering value to its users. Management does their job when they eliminate impediments. The Team does its job when it meets its commitments as described in each Sprint's Backlog.

In other words, in Scrum, the team is both *empowered and accountable* to deliver the goods. The team does their job when they self-organize, self-manage and self-achieve the objectives of the Sprint. For many organizations, this turns things upside down. The hierarchical-technical-management-directive approach is essentially eliminated with Scrum. The Product Owner now sets the objectives and priorities, the team figures out how to achieve them, and no one need tell them how to do that along the way.

1.2.1.3 Better, Though Less Predictable Outcomes vs. False Confidence Scrum starts with the premise that creating software is a complicated business operating in a highly-fluid and technical environment, and that no one can reliably predict or definitively plan exactly what a team will deliver, when they will deliver it, and what the quality and cost will be. Instead, Scrum understands that teams can estimate these items, communicate the estimates, negotiate a near term plan according to various risks and then adjust as they proceed. The agreement is that the team *will deliver the best possible software given the circumstances*, and that following any cookbook approach won't improve the definition of "best," and will only hinder the team's responsiveness to the real-world complexity and unpredictability that exists.

Historically, ignoring this philosophy creates a number of organizational problems:

- Management actually believes that it can predict the cost, delivery schedule, and functionality that will be delivered, and plans accordingly.
- Developers and project managers are forced to live a lie: they pretend they can plan, predict and deliver. They build one way, but must pretend they build another way. In the end, they are essentially without controls.
- By the time the system is delivered, it is often irrelevant or requires significant change. A key cause is that high iteration costs limit our visibility into the usefulness of what the team is actually developing, until it is too late.

Recognizing these realities is not without its challenges – for example, what manager wants to tell their executive they don't know exactly *what* the team will deliver on the given date? But the benefits of this approach are that organizations are truly empowered: the business is finally free to produce better outcomes for its end users and will now do so more quickly, clearly creating competitive advantage for the business.

1.2.2 Scrum and Software Agility

Scrum has been in use since the mid 1990s and has now been applied to thousands of projects worldwide. In addition to Scrum, several new iterative methodologies have also received attention during this period. Like Scrum, each had a combination of old ideas and new ideas, but they *all* emphasized:

- Close collaboration between the development team and business experts;
- Face-to-face communication (as more efficient than written documentation);
- Frequent delivery of new deployable business value software;
- Transparency of intentions, progress, and artifacts;
- Tight, self-organizing teams; and
- Ways to craft the code and the team to allow for continuous adaptation to changing requirements.

In 2001, various originators and practitioners of these methodologies, including Scrum leaders, met to understand what it was they had in common.

They picked the word "agile" for an umbrella term and crafted the "Manifesto for Agile Software Development", its most important aspect being a statement of shared values:

> *We are uncovering better ways of developing software by doing it and helping others do it. Through this work we have come to value:*
>
> ■ Individuals and interactions over processes and tools
> ■ Working software over comprehensive documentation
> ■ Customer collaboration over contract negotiation
> ■ Responding to change over following a plan
>
> *That is, while there is value in the items on the right, we value the items on the left more.*

The Manifesto struck a chord and it led to the start of thousands of new agile projects. The results and experiences of these projects further enhanced the techniques applied by the multiple forms of agile practices. As with any human endeavor, some succeeded and some failed. But what was most striking about the successes was how much both the business people and the technical people loved their project. This was the way they wanted software development done – and the customers and end users agreed. Successful projects spawned more enthusiasts and like a successful Sprint, the virtuous agile cycle continues today.

1.3 Preparing for Scrum

Once CXOs have a basic understanding of the business and cultural benefits of Scrum and agility, they often want to take the next step and see how this development method can improve their organization.

During its first fifteen years of life, most Scrum implementations have been driven bottom-up. In other words, a project team would try Scrum and the results would be impressive. Another team would try it, and pretty soon Scrum projects appear throughout the organization. More recently, however, many organizations want to implement Scrum top-down as part of a directive to speed the company's responsiveness and to improve productivity.

Since Scrum is all about team empowerment and "letting the team decide," a top down implementation requires thoughtful consideration and preparation, as we will describe in this section.

1.3.1 "Scrumming" both the Software Process and the Organization

Many organizations have tolerated inefficiencies and impediments for years; Scrum quickly identifies these and requires their resolution. Fortunately, the increased productivity and value derived from Scrum projects makes the effort worthwhile, but it is still an effort.

To implement Scrum, an organization has to take on two pieces of work. Firstly, projects where development teams are taught to build software-using Scrum; and, secondly, removing the impediments to optimized creation and delivery of software that the Scrum teams encounter. The first work improves software delivery; the second remedies impediments to ROI and productivity identified in the first.

Both pieces of work are challenging and require hard work above and beyond the actual development of software; a full Scrum implementation may take up to five years. No matter the intensity or commitment by management, this timetable cannot be rushed because the core of the project is organizational change.

Scrum's daily and monthly inspection and adaptation cycles make everything visible - the code, the process, and the company's impediments. Projects using Scrum regularly identify impediments that must be recorded, evaluated, prioritized, and acted upon.

The speed of Scrum implementation is directly related to the:

- Degree of change required within the organization;
- Urgency within the organization to improve its software development and delivery process;
- Effectiveness of leadership within the organization.

1.3.2 The CXO's Role as Organizational Scrum Master
for Continuous Improvement

In Scrum, the *Scrum Master* is responsible for making sure a Scrum team lives by the values and practices of Scrum. The Scrum Master protects the team by making sure they do not over-commit themselves to what they can achieve during a Sprint and the Scrum Master continuously removes impediments that prevent the team from successfully delivering the Sprint results.

The CXO is the Scrum Master for Organizational Change

At the organizational-impediment level, this job falls to the CXO or other executive sponsor, whose job it is to work outside the team and eliminate the organizational barriers that may prevent the success of an agile development model.

The job of the *Organizational Scrum Master* is to notice, identify, and work within the organization to cause change that removes impediments. That is, the CXO as Organizational Scrum Master is primarily a change agent, and the list of impediments is their Product Backlog. The CXO's Scrum sponsor – acting as "Product Owner" for these impediments – sets the priorities of these items. This Product Backlog of impediments is worked on by the organization through teams using the Scrum process, with deliverables being impediment removal. This organizational change backlog starts during the pilot projects and continues as long as needed changes are identified during the inspect-and-adapt cycle of Scrum.

The Organizational Scrum Master periodically meets with all of the Scrum Masters, product owner and sponsor to further develop the Organizational Change Product Backlog. Teams are formed that drive changes to the organization within a Sprint. At the Sprint Review, the change is reviewed as well as the metric that can be used to monitor progress in implementing the change. In this way, the CXO engages in a process of continued organizational improvement all aimed specifically at increasing the productivity and quality of the software development teams.

1.3.3 Caution: Change is Hard Work

Change is hard work and there is no way around the hard work. Organizations implementing Scrum sometimes misidentify the hard work as someone's fault, something that can be made to go away if the group at fault would just "clean up their act". This type of organizational blame can kill a Scrum implementation, and with it the organization's ability to build better software. When something is painful, when something goes wrong, recognize this is just part of the change that is occurring; it is an opportunity for everyone to get together to figure out how to solve the problem, together.

Scrum cannot be planned for and implemented with checklists, procedures, and forms. Scrum is just a simple framework that will identify everything in an organization that gets in the way of optimally building software. The work to manage and remove these impediments represents the difficult part of implementing Scrum, and it is different for every organization, since every organization is different.

Nobody likes pain and difficulty; many of the impediments are so inherent to an organization's way of thinking and operating that they are very difficult to remove. No amount of planning up front will mitigate this difficulty; it will only help alert everyone to the hard work that must be done to become a world-class competitor. Scrum requires that senior management be vitally involved in impediment triage and removal, and therefore requires that the CXO adopting Scrum become the *leading agent for change*.

In this way, the CXO engages in a process of continued organizational improvement, all aimed at increasing the productivity and quality of the software teams. It's not easy, and the leadership the CXO provides will be a critical factor in success, as the following note from Ken Schwaber to a CEO illustrates:

From: Ken Schwaber
To: XXX XXXXX, CEO for XXXXXXX Corporation

"On one hand, Scrum offers some very attractive possibilities – increased productivity, a better working environment, increased competitiveness, and a higher quality product. On the other hand, it is hard to implement. The amount of change engendered by a Scrum implementation is significant and difficult.

Even though the change is difficult for the developers and customers (product owners), they have immediate payback through increased job satisfaction. This helps them through times of stress and anxiety. Middle management, however, is stressed without immediate reward. They are asked to help transition an organization from traditional approaches to leaner approaches without a clear vision of a personal end point . . . what will I do and where will I fit into the new organization. This question is particularly difficult and fraught with danger since middle management will be fashioning the new organization. The potential for conflict and politics is daunting.

My experience with top-down, enterprise implementations of Scrum has led me to believe that the differentiator between success and failure is you. Your ability to vision the future and help communicate it to your management, your ability to patiently guide them through the change, and your ability to assure your middle management of their value and form them into a team will differentiate your ability to absorb the change and realize the benefits, or not."

1.4 A Playbook for Adopting Scrum

Once you decide to implement Scrum within your organization, a journey begins with a belief that the effort will be rewarded with a more effective software process and a more responsive and competitive company. It also recognizes that a significant amount of organizational change is now in the forecast.

As the CXO contemplates this undertaking, an understanding of organizational behavior leads to a rational set of steps for achieving substantive change. These include:

- Finding an evangelist and local sponsor;
- Taking small initial steps that test the waters;
- Reflecting on successes and failures, then moving forward, step by step.

This next section describes some typical examples of how you might implement Scrum throughout your organization; a "playbook" that gives sample techniques you can apply to accomplish the requisite change.

1.4.1 Play 0 – Overview, Assessment and Pilot Preparation

The objective of the first play is to prepare the playing field for the activities ahead by a) assessing the organizations readiness for agility, b) providing initial training for the early participants and c) building the Product Backlog for the initial projects. The details of this play are as follows:

(i) Overview and Assessment
Description: Two day working session consisting of
  o Scrum Aptitude Test – exposes management to the types of change that happen with Scrum, and help them determine if they want to proceed.
  o Scrum presentations – raise general awareness and present concepts to entire organization.
  o Assess organizational readiness and define next steps.
  o Define plans; identify potential pilots, schedule training, and resource the pilot project.
  o Dinner with senior management to review next steps.

Duration: 2 days

Support: External

(ii) Pilot Preparation

The organization is ready to proceed with the training and structure needed to support the first pilot project. Activities in this phase include:

Scrum Master training
> Description: Train Scrum Masters to run the pilots
> Duration: 2 days
> Support: External

Product Owner training
> Description: Train Product Owners to maximize ROI using Scrum.
> Duration: 2 days
> Support: External

Team (Developer) training
> Description: Train all Team members to work as a cross-functional, self-organizing Team that delivers "done" increments of functionality with modern engineering practices on a specific technology stack.
> Duration: 5 days
> Support: External

Establish Metrics
> Description: Review and modify metrics that monitor the use of Scrum within the organization and define the value derived from the pilots. Establish core Scrum process and project metrics.
> Duration: 1 week
> Support: External

Establish Change Product Backlog
> Description: Establish product backlog for tracking and evaluating impediments that arise during the pilot projects. This backlog will be the basis for change action within the organization.
> Duration: 1 day
> Support: External

1.4.2 Play 1 - Pilot Project(s)

The objective of this play is to experience Scrum on one or more real projects in order to demonstrate the positive benefits of improved software agility within the organization. One or more pilot projects are now executed. Scrum Masters and management closely watch the pilots to identify organizational obstacles and impediments to Scrum. When these impediments are identified, they are fixed on the spot where possible, or are simply recorded in the Organizational Change Backlog and categorized for later attention.

(i) Pilot projects
Duration: 3-6 months

Support: External/Internal Scrum Master

Description: Run 3 to 6 iterations of the pilot projects. Pilot projects deliver increments of functionality and identify impediments to optimized software development. Assess and adjust plan, evaluate and prioritize impediments.

(ii) Retrospective
Duration: 2 day

Support: External/Internal Scrum Master
Description: Review pilot projects, metrics, and impediments. Assess what went right, what could be improved. Identify the ROI. Assess impact on business operations, including relationships within organizational departments and with customers.

(iii) Re-planning
Duration: 1 day

Support: External/Internal Scrum Master
Description: Modify master plan for Scrum implementation; keep it high level and let project plans and the organizational change plan be driven by their own specific product backlogs.

1.4.3 Play 2 – Organizational Expansion

Based on successful pilots, the objective of this play is to expand the usage of Scrum and its benefits to a significant subset of the development organization.

By now, there is an understanding of what beneficial practices are embedded, what impediments stand in the way of broader adoption and where further training is required. For example, the following broader training programs may now be effective:

- Scrum Master training: Before scaling the implementation to additional and larger projects you must be increase the number of Scrum Masters. Candidates with appropriate skills should now be recognized in the organization. Scrum Masters who will be leading Scrum of Scrums (see below) can now be trained in advanced skills like Team Facilitation and Metrics Collection.
- Product Owner Training: Customers and Product Managers will learn a way to optimize return-on-investment while managing commitments and risks. The will learn to do this through the role of the Product Owner, who is responsible for managing progress to optimize value and avoid surprises.
- Developer Training: The developers involved in agile projects will have to learn to operate as self-organizing, cross-functional Teams that deliver complete increments of functionality using modern engineering practices on specified technology stacks.
- Scrum/Agility training: a successful implementation of Scrum will largely depend on a common vocabulary of all people involved. This can be achieved through 2 – 4 hour introduction courses for 30-50% of the organization.

In addition, you may apply other activities to increase the visibility and level of acceptance of Scrum in the organization:

- Information radiators: Communicate the state of Scrum projects through simple and powerful information radiators, like whiteboards showing the tasks (Task Board), Product and Release Backlogs and the project and program BurnDown charts.
- Reading: A suggestion of articles and books can be provided to all people in the organization to encourage further knowledge expansion.
- CXO led seminars/brownbags: The change leader(s) should communicate often and openly about what is happening in the organization. Informal meetings, like brownbags and pizza hours tend to have a positive impact on change.

■ Chats/war stories/feedback from the pilot(s): The results from the pilot projects should be available to everybody. This will increase discussion and involvement through all levels of the organization.

1.4.4 Play 3 – Achieving Impact

As the pilot projects have proven that real value will be delivered through an agile approach to software development, the objective of this play is to achieve a more significant impact on the bottom line, which can only be demonstrated through more and larger projects. Through the previous plays the organization has collected sufficient explicit and tacit knowledge to be able to tackle these with a high probability for success. At this point, as much as 25% of the organization should be involved in the implementation of Scrum.

Effective change should now be occurring inside and outside the development organization. Inside development, the work is best done by the development team. Outside the development teams, the work of eliminating impediments is directed by the Organizational Scrum Master and is implemented by the affected departments.

(i) Development Projects

Duration: Forever

Support: Internal

Description: Development projects monitored by ROI.

(ii) Change Projects

Duration: Most work in first 1 to 2 years; then, as needed

Support: Internal

Description: Organizational change projects within various departments drive out emerging and changing impediments.

(iii) Assess and Adapt

Duration: Every Sprint

Support: External/Internal Scrum Master

Description: Review qualitative and quantitative metrics. Add additional metrics and review how metrics are captured whenever a surprise has occurred.

1.4.5 Play 4 – Measure, Assess and Adjust

The objective of this play is to assess the organization's progress and to establish a broader set of metrics to serve as a basis for further expansion. The CXO should be aware that the upcoming discussion of metrics may be both controversial and entertaining as many of the traditional metrics that might be in place prior to Scrum adoption (example: measures of "document completeness") are no longer relevant. Fortunately, Scrum and agile practices are indeed accountable and measurable and practitioners are converging on a set of metrics that provide qualitative and quantitative feedback at both the process and project level.

But before entering this discussion, a *key distinction* needs to be made between many traditional software development processes and Scrum and agile:

The primary metric for agile software development is whether or not working software actually exists, and is demonstrably suitable for use in its intended purpose. In Scrum, that key indicator is determined empirically, by demonstration, **at the end of every single Sprint***.*

This primary measure of software quality and productivity is the essence of agile development. So with Scrum, you cannot be very far off your objective without knowing that you are. All other metrics are subordinate to that objective and its constant mantra of *"delivering working software more frequently"*.

At this point in the Scrum adoption game, a significant part of the organization is now operating in an agile manner. Sprint results of the initial projects are the primary measure of the effectiveness of the new team behaviors and their new processes. This data should be published and analyzed.

Moreover, now is the appropriate time to define a set of secondary metrics used to guide your organization on how it implements Scrum. In so doing, there are two types of metrics that may be applied:

Process Metrics – primarily qualitative indicators on the effectiveness of the teams and organization in adopting Scrum. These include items such as effectiveness of the teams in managing the Product Backlog, effectiveness of Scrum processes such as the Scrum daily meeting, Sprint Planning meeting, etc.

Project Metrics – At the project level, an additional set of metrics may be applied to measure the results for a particular Scrum team and the service, component or system that they are accountable for. These may include some traditional metrics such as defect count, percentage of code with unit test coverage, percentage of code covered by automated regression tests, etc., as well as Scrum specific metrics such as number of user stories finished and demonstrable at the end of each Sprint.

A Note on Quality and Scrum

Customers often pressure development organizations to deliver features faster than is feasible. Some organizations accommodate this by reducing the quality of the product, dropping re-factoring, cutting test efforts and other solid engineering practices. This is not supportable within Scrum practices since the system or product is a corporate asset, refined continuously and objectively measured, not a one-time project asset. Engineering organizations that succumb to this pressure eventually build "design dead" systems that can not be effectively maintained or enhanced. The organization suffers the huge cost of a substantial rewrite and re-release of the code base. To avoid this, only the senior levels of an organization can make an asset decision for reducing quality.

1.4.6 Play 5 – Expand and Win

With these activities behind the organization, and with a defined set of metrics to guide and evaluate future progress on an organization-wide basis, it is now time to expand the use of Scrum across the entire organization. The activities in this phase of the implementation are focused on the further scaling of Scrum within the organization.

In steps of perhaps 25–30% of head count, the remaining teams in the organization are introduced to Scrum. Existing practices are further refined and shared between the teams in order to reach an organizational inculcation of the agile practices. Only now can the strict rules with which Scrum operates be adjusted to better match the need of the organization. Customers can be invited to participate in the implementation through training as product owners or Scrum Masters. This phase will continue until all teams are involved in

Scrum, and Scrum's inspect-and-adapt mechanisms will address further enhancement of your processes and practices.

At this point, the organization will be receiving the substantial productivity and business and cultural benefits of Scrum.

Before we proceed to Scaling Scrum to the largest project environments, however, we need to look at the types of organizational impediments that can prevent effective Scrum practices.

1.5 Organizational Impediments to Adopting Scrum

Applications developed in any organization are intended to optimize the ability of the company to meet its business mission. However, over the course of time, organizations evolve in ways which are not always conducive to the productivity of the software team that develops and maintains those applications. Indeed, some organizations have evolved to the point where the software practices are largely dysfunctional and – despite repeated efforts to improve them – the organizational structure, policies and strictures prevent effective change. This section describes the source and nature of these impediments to better arm the CXO for the work ahead.

1.5.1 Exposing the Impediments with Scrum

The very nature of Scrum; its incessant demands for quality software to be delivered more quickly; its continuous demand for working with end users to assure effective implementation, and its continuous inspection and adaptation mechanisms expose dysfunctional practices and "blocking issues" very quickly. This ef-

> It's impossible to identify all the organizational efforts up front.

fect becomes all the more pronounced when Scrum is also used as a process to implement and scale Scrum in the organization.

You cannot identify all impediments up front as they are embedded in the organization and therefore too familiar to be identified easily. Only when you start using Scrum do they become obvious. The plan for implementation emerges as the evidence of what needs to be changed and the organization's *willingness to make the change* emerges.

1.5.2 Characterizing Impediments

Impediments will generally be encountered in four areas:

Scrum Process Itself – what impediments are occurring that get in the way of the Scrum process?

People Practices – what people practices are getting in the way of developing, distributing, supporting and using products to maximize the fulfillment of everyone involved?

Product Engineering Practices – what practices are impeding the optimization of return on investment, or maximizing the mission of the organization from a product perspective, and what impediments are there to optimized product development and delivery?

Organizational Issues – what systemic organizational issues – that lie clearly outside the team's control – are preventing the teams from delivering software to its users more quickly?

We want separate categories in the Organizational Impediment Product Backlog because these require unique skills to resolve. In addition, they should be prioritized as to impact, and some thought should be given as to who best in the organization can best resolve the impediment.

1.6 Scaling Scrum

The business benefits of Scrum and agility are most readily achieved with small, co-located and integrated teams, ideally consisting of eleven people or less (including Product Owner, Scrum Master, and Team (of Developers)) and where each Scrum team owns a specific product or application that they can define, develop, test and deliver without much outside help.

Inevitably, however, the success of Scrum will lead to its application to larger programs, systems of systems, and applications that take many, likely distributed, teams to develop and deliver. Fortunately, Scrum has been proven in projects consisting of many hundreds of developers so Scrum does scale to the challenge of the larger software enterprise. Doing so, however, brings about a unique set of challenges that must be addressed, specifically:

1. Scaling the organization: Scrum teams of teams
2. Tooling infrastructure for enterprise agility
3. Coordinating teams of teams

Each of these challenges is addressed in the sections below.

1.6.1 Scaling the Organization: Scrum Teams of Teams

Consistent with its less is more philosophy, Scrum has a very small number of rules. However, most of the rules that do exist are fixed and relatively inviolate. One basic rule is the team consists of eleven or fewer members. These team should, whenever possible, be collocated in a common work area. This is the most effective and productive model as it a) supports the requirement for constant informal communication amongst the team members, b) fosters a high degree of esprit de corps and c) allows for a mutual commitment to the goals of the Sprint amongst team members who actually know each other and have to work together every day. In addition, certain Scrum mechanisms, such as Sprint planning and the Daily Scrum meeting can breakdown very quickly as the team size gets beyond 8-10 individuals. Reasons for not collocating teams or having oversized teams should be cost-justified.

Scaling Scrum to larger applications (as shown in Figure A3.2) leaves this key principle in place. So, scaling to an application involving 300 people involves organizing around 30 Scrum teams. As previously discussed, the team's complement must be fully rounded and capable of developing potentially shippable pieces of functionality at every Sprint. For most organizations, this requires reorganizing teams around product features, services, components or subsystems, rather than by individual role (e.g. developer pool, test resources, etc.). While we discussed this organizational impediment earlier, we see it gets compounded as our project's size increases.

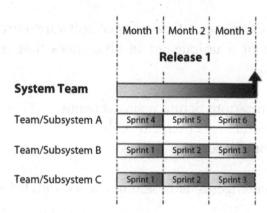

Figure A3.2   A System Being Built by Three Scrum Teams Over Three Sprints

Organization Follows Architecture

Moreover, we cannot readily form Scrum teams without understanding how each individual team can relatively holistically deliver end user functionality. In turn, this mandates that we decompose the application architecture into components or subsystems that have conceptual integrity and can deliver business value on their own[1]. Scrum provides for this architectural factoring activity in the Sprint staging phase, and in early Sprints, by the front-running Scrum teams. This method works particularly well in a period of Scrum expansion and rollout for a large project. Here, the front-running teams build proof points of customer value while they simultaneously factor the application architecture to accept additional teams, whose Scrum training will likely be occurring at about the same time. As each new team is formed, its role in the larger system becomes clear and a picture like Figure A3.2 emerges.

1.6.2 Coordinating Teams of Teams

Of course, the presence of a large number of teams brings significant challenges in coordinating and communicating across teams, and also implies that there will likely be a number of issues at the system level which require the

---

[1] This level of sharing and communication can indeed be a challenge when implementing service oriented architectures, as the existing organization likely mirrors the prior architecture of independent silos of applications whose department owners were not overly-required to cooperate to deliver more flexible services to users, as now becomes the case.

same daily and monthly inspection practices applied at the local team level. Experiences with scaling Scrum to larger teams have evolved a small set of useful practices for coordinating disparate teams and addressing the larger challenges of Sprint planning, release planning and tracking system level integration and test activities.

Daily Communication: Scrum of Scrums

In the same fashion that Scrum mandates daily communication in the daily Scrum, larger and distributed teams typically coordinate their activities in a daily Scrum of Scrums. In this meeting, team leaders from each component team use the same format as the single team daily meeting:

1. What did my team do yesterday to advance the objectives of the Sprint?
2. What will my team do today?
3. What impediments are present that could keep my team from meeting its commitment to the Sprint?

Ideally, this meeting occurs immediately after the individual team's daily Scrum. When teams are dispersed, it often occurs by telephone with the time of day selected to maximize participation amongst the scrum of scrum team members.

(ii) System Level Release Planning and Tracking Figure A3.2 might imply that it is a fairly straightforward matter to divide the organization into feature, service or subsystem teams, empower these teams to do their jobs, and that a wonderfully integrated system will naturally occur. Experience has shown that this is unlikely. For even when the individual teams are empowered to meet both the needs of the Sprint and coordinate integration between the teams/subsystems, a larger set of challenges is present. That is the challenge of building a system holistically, where we implement ant test our integrations across all subsystems, where subsystems work together to meet broader customer requirements and that the overall system meets its quality, performance and reliability requirements. We now require that for any team's work to be considered complete, the integrated, integration tested work of all teams must be complete. This is shown in Figure A3.3.

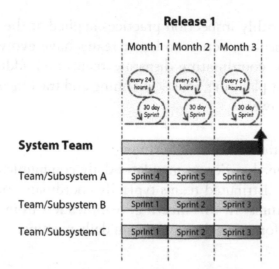

Figure A3.3   System of Three Subsystems with System Level Sprints

To address these challenges, many teams have added a technical lead role played at the system level. Architects, team leads, product managers and quality assurance personnel will often grow into an additional Scrum team to think and act at the system level. Moreover, they can also apply the Scrum process at the system level to set Sprint objectives and create backlog items of forced system integrations, system level demonstrations, quality checkpoints, trial distributions and other milestones to assure that the system stays on track. In so doing, the picture in Figure A3.3 starts to emerge.

1.6.3 Tooling Infrastructure for Enterprise Agility

Even with this level of structure and coordination, larger projects and distributed teams may still find themselves lacking the internal and cross-team coordination and project visibility required to reliably deliver software in rapid, fully-tested iterations. While Scrum provides a proven framework for the project management aspects of software development, it does not prescribe specific software engineering practices nor recommend specific tooling to support the Scrum process. Scrum's philosophy in this regard is "keep it simple and let the teams decide." As organizations have struggled with modern engineering practices, Scrum.org has introduced Scrum Developer programs and training oriented around modern Application LifeCycle Management tooling.

Indeed, for the ideal team of less than ten co-located persons, the prime project management artifacts used to plan the Sprint and communicate status of individual features, tasks and team progress can often be managed using a spreadsheet developed and maintained by the Scrum Master. The engineering artifacts for requirements, test cases and defects may be equally lightweight and written on index cards, whiteboards or maintained on a team wiki.

People and Communication

However, scaling Scrum practices to distributed teams, and teams of teams, presents special communication challenges. Cross-team coordination of how to implement shared requirements, track feature status and identify blocking issues becomes a primary concern. In these cases *"a mechanism for frequently synchronizing*

> Scaling Scrum presents special communication challenges

their work must be devised and implemented. Also, a more detailed product and technical architecture must be constructed so the work can be cleanly divided across teams." (Schwaber 2004)

While traditional project management tools may have worked for showing idealized task start/stop dates and performing – perhaps fruitless – critical path analysis on long waterfall projects, these plan-driven activities lose their relevance when working in short iterations where the entire team focuses on driving the few highest priority features to acceptance. Instead of one person maintaining a separate task database that is decoupled from the day-to-day artifacts the team is actually planning and implementing (e.g. user stories and tests), larger programs need a real-time collaboration environment that supports the natural signaling occurring among team members as they advance a feature from the Product Backlog into development, testing and integration. To emulate the co-located team, this agile project management environment must let everyone quickly see and update where a feature is in its lifecycle, how much effort remains before its completion and what specific issues are blocking its progress.

Besides needing new ways to plan and track our iterations, the capabilities of tools applied to defining, organizing and sharing our system artifacts have new demands as well. Managing requirements, their acceptance tests and defects calls for support that is horizontal across the lifecycle activities inside a Sprint, not vertical with deep silos of artifact information that are poorly related to the commitments the teams have made. In fact, with rapid itera-tions, it is really the relationships between these artifacts that are the primary concern to the teams. After all, each Sprint is producing many pieces of work-ing, tested code, so the teams must understand exactly how these engineering artifacts relate to each other and be able to see their status at every point in time.

Tooling Infrastructure Opportunities

Being software developers after all, the teams will naturally want to better organize their artifacts and automate those aspects of the Scrum process that lend themselves to software support. Specifically, the teams will likely want to add infrastructure support for the following activities and artifact types in the software lifecycle:

- **Backlog Management** – As system complexity grows, the team will want better support for capture and maintenance of the feature lists, functional and nonfunctional requirements, use cases, and user stories as well as the priorities, estimates, status and owners of these items. As Scrum is applied to larger proj-ects, these artifacts may grow to many thousands in count and a means to organize, support and view them by system or subsystem becomes critical.
- **Project Reporting** – Scrum eschews traditional, waterfall-like project *plans*, but the tactical day to day *project management* nature of Scrum is in-tense and unremitting. The team will need a simple way for each member to enter their task estimates, status, and effort remaining so that the Burn-Down Charts are automated and continuously available. In addition, the infrastructure should support the natural signaling teams use as backlog items move through their lifecycle. Senior personnel will need to look across teams and understand their individual iterations and release plans in order to asses the status of their program as a whole.
- **Just-in-Time Requirements Elaboration** – Many smaller Scrum projects succeed with informal requirements mechanisms such as direct discussion between the Product Owner and Team, but as project complexity and criticality grows, more depth and richness of requirements expression and requirements versioning will likely be required. For example, documenta-tion of interfaces that affect multiple teams becomes critical. Changes to interfaces or new features that cross team boundaries may have a

significant impact on the project. These requirements should be elaborated on a just-in-time basis, meaning at, or just prior to the Sprint that implements the new functionality. To address this problem, teams may want centralized support for richer forms of requirements expression, their compilation for review and automated change notification.

- **Early Testing** – Since every Sprint delivers potentially shippable code into the product baseline, early test case development and test automation enables teams to support the rapid iteration requirements of Scrum. Tooling that generates test cases directly from requirements or story cards will accelerate the development process and provide the inherent traceability needed to prove acceptance of the feature. Know that the ongoing management of the hundreds and thousands of regression tests that accrue will likely become the critical factor in determining the speed and success of your Sprints.

- **Release Planning** – The philosophy of Scrum focuses on the "art of the possible in the nearer term", as opposed to the black art of supposedly predicting exactly what will be delivered 6-12 Sprints down the road. This philosophy is a breakthrough in thinking at the team level because it allows Scrum teams to focus in a "heads down" fashion for 30 days at a time, and thus produce working software more reliably. But as the teams grow and scale, applying additional analysis and rigor to Sprints beyond the immediate horizon helps avoid architectures that require substantial re-factoring down the road. While re-factoring is highly encouraged in agile, it becomes less practical as the scope of the application and the number of existing deployments increases. Additional release planning that provides us with architectural runway is often appropriate. Therefore, the art of Sprint planning can include "a few Sprints out" and "what-if" planning functions that help the teams make backlog tradeoffs and communicate a reasonable vision and product roadmap to the sponsors.

In addition, these teams will typically want to organize all these assets in a central repository where every team member can access them, *24x7, worldwide*, and one which provides instantaneous views of project and program status, with automated change notification for critical project changes.

(iii) Evolving the Infrastructure in Sprints In Scrum, deploying this level of infrastructure is not a one time event, done "up front" by a tooling team.

Instead, the Scrum teams themselves take on the task of identifying what they will buy and build to address their problems based on the lessons learned in prior Sprints. Moreover, these investments are made in the context of ongoing Sprints. Therefore the team addresses the build out of infrastructure by adding items to the Product Backlog to address the infrastructure items as per Figure A3.4 below. Of course, customer facing functionality still takes priority, but the experienced team recognizes they must be able to continuously schedule infrastructure work as well in order to maintain their velocity and productivity as the application scope and number of teams grows.

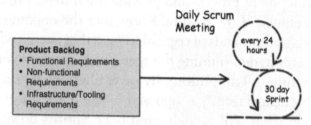

Figure A3.4 Parsing Scalability Infrastructure into a Sprint

1.7 Summary

Scrum is a proven and effective software development practice that can rapidly increase the productivity, delivery speed and quality of software teams.

What development organization would not benefit from these attributes commonly experienced by successful Scrum implementations?

- Decreased development cycle times
- Higher value throughput to end users
- Higher quality
- Lower development risk
- Greater user satisfaction
- Improved company morale

While appearing simple on the surface, implementing Scrum often requires substantial organizational change to eliminate the impediments to effective development and delivery. As lead change agent, the CXO or other executive sponsor has the primary responsibility for eliminating these impediments. It is the enduring commitment by the CXO that may well be the difference between success and failure of the implementation. While none of this is easy, the CXO who commits to improving software outcomes with Scrum will take the first step in ensuring that the enterprise is well on its way to achieving the business benefits of faster and better quality software delivery.

In addition, Scrum is highly effective in large-scale enterprise application development and can support the needs of many hundreds of developers working on shared applications. Scaling Scrum presents an additional set of challenges to infrastructure and tooling that the teams themselves will address – but overcoming these challenges will likely deliver a substantial advantage to these larger organizations over their marketplace rivals.

Index